EMERGING HEROES

WWII-Era Diplomats, Jewish Refugees, and Escape to Japan

A Story in 7 Photographs

EMERGING HEROES

WWII-Era Diplomats, Jewish Refugees, and Escape to Japan

A Story in 7 Photographs

Akira Kitade

Translated by **Kuniko Katz** and
Edited by **Donna Ratajczak**

BOSTON
2022

Library of Congress Cataloging-in-Publication Data

Names: Kitade, Akira, 1944- author. | Katz, Kuniko, translator. | Ratajczak, Donna, editor.

Title: Emerging heroes : WWII-Era Diplomats, Jewish refugees, and escape to Japan. A story in 7 photographs / Akira Kitade ; translated by Kuniko Katz and edited by Donna Ratajczak.

Other titles: Inochi no biza, haruka naru tabiji. English | Story of the Japanese saviors of Jewish WWII refugees through 7 photographs

Description: Boston : Academic Studies Press, 2022. | Series: Judaism and Jewish life | Includes bibliographical references.

Identifiers: LCCN 2022012405 (print) | LCCN 2022012406 (ebook) | ISBN 9781644698686 (hardback) | ISBN 9781644698693 (paperback) | ISBN 9781644698709 (adobe pdf) | ISBN 9781644698716 (epub)

Subjects: LCSH: World War, 1939-1945--Jews--Rescue--Japan. | Righteous Gentiles in the Holocaust--Japan. | Sugihara, Chiune, 1900-1986. | World War, 1939-1945--Jews--Rescue--Lithuania--Kaunas.

Classification: LCC D804.6 .K5713 2022 (print) | LCC D804.6 (ebook) | DDC 940.53/180952--dc23/eng/20220328

LC record available at https://lccn.loc.gov/2022012405
LC ebook record available at https://lccn.loc.gov/2022012406

ISBN 9781644698686 (hardback)
ISBN 9781644698693 (paperback)
ISBN 9781644698709 (adobe pdf)
ISBN 9781644698716 (epub)

Book design by Kryon Publishing Services, www.kryonpublishing.com/
Cover design by Ivan Grave
Published by Academic Studies Press
1577 Beacon Street
Brookline, MA 02446, USA
press@academicstudiespress.com
www.academicstudiespress.com

Contents

Message from the Mayor of Tsuruga City

Congratulations on the publication of the new book *Emerging Heroes: WWII-Era Diplomats, Jewish Refugees, and Escape to Japan—A Story in 7 Photographs.*

Who could have imagined that the seven photos, taken seventy years ago, would lead us to such an epic journey?

This book expresses the author's affection for people whom he met, with admiration for his superior Mr. Tatsuo Osako and the Japanese people who communicated with refugees at that time such as the staff of Japan Tourist Bureau. The interviews conducted on the families of those who appear in these photos and Sugihara Survivors tell us their lives and feelings.

The author wrote also about other diplomats besides Mr. Sugihara, and this expands his epic journey. I sincerely look forward to Mr. Kitade's continued success as a reader and a friend of his.

The album Mr. Osako left was donated to Tsuruga City through the kindness of Mr. Osako's family and Mr. Kitade. I'd be very happy if you could visit our "Port of Humanity Tsuruga Museum" to enjoy its exhibition.

Takanobu Fuchikami
Mayor, Tsuruga City

Foreword

The legacy of Japanese diplomat Chiune Sugihara is one that might have easily been forgotten, if not for the survivors themselves coming forward and recognizing his humanitarian effort. Sugihara defied orders because he saw a moral obligation and issued over 2,000 life-saving travel visas. As a result, he rescued thousands of Jews. His legacy lives on in their progeny today.

Sugihara's courageous actions alone could not have delivered those Jewish refugees all the way from Kaunas, Lithuania to safety in Kobe, Japan. Travel visas required an end destination, outside of Japan, and many countries had closed their doors to Jewish refugees. In addition, many of these Jews were impoverished, with no money to support the journey. The refugees were able to reach safety and survive the Holocaust, thanks to crucial support received from many individuals and organizations.

Even eighty years after these actions, we are privileged to be able to continue to learn further details of Sugihara's life-saving visas, as well as the roles of other courageous, selfless individuals. The research efforts undertaken by Akira Kitade portray tenacity and dedication to preserving history. I am grateful to him for shining a spotlight on key diplomats from Japan, as well as from the Netherlands and Poland, who were critical to the rescue of so many refugees—and to the many survivors for sharing their personal stories. It is inspiring to learn of courageous individuals who stood for righteousness in a time of such bleakness in human history.

As President of the American Jewish Committee (AJC), I'm proud that the American Jewish community, too, was instrumental in facilitating the survival of Sugihara's visa-holders. American Jews did critical work in fundraising and advocating for these individuals, many of whom eventually immigrated to the United States and contributed to Jewish life in America. I had the opportunity to meet Rick Salomon, the son of a Sugihara visa-holder, whose story is captured within these pages. I met him in January 2017 when he gave a keynote address in New York City. I also had the pleasure of reading his son Mark's essay, which is excerpted in this book.

My own family's history was not so lucky. My parents survived the concentration camp. My father was the sole survivor of his family, and my mother lost her mother and siblings, save for one. Had they had the protection of such courageous diplomats as are portrayed in this book, their wartime experience might have taken a different turn.

Today, the need for American Jewish engagement in global issues remains, and as a community, we continue to respond to this call. There are many lessons we can learn from the actions of Chiune Sugihara and others who aided the effort to rescue the Jewish refugees fleeing the Holocaust. AJC strives to follow the spirit of Sugihara, not only in helping global Jewry, but also by helping many others throughout the world who are in need.

As we build with others a world with less hate and more understanding, respect, and peace, I am grateful for such accounts as Akira Kitade's *Emerging Heroes: WWII-Era Diplomats, Jewish Refugees, and Escape to Japan—A Story in 7 Photographs*, which inspire and energize us along the way.

Harriet P. Schleifer
President, American Jewish Committee

Acknowledgments

Despite the difficulties brought about by COVID-19, I was fortunate enough to have been able to publish the original Japanese version of this book in December 2020.

It is also fortunate that thanks to the warm encouragement of many people its English translation has been made possible in less than a year. I would like to thank the following individuals for their assistance and contributions presented in these chapters.

Chapter 2

Mr. Paul Hamer, Mr. David Manski, Prof. Charles Manski, Ms. Karen Leon, Mr. Damon Krukowski, Mr. Mark Salomon, Mr. Junichi Kajioka

Chapter 3

Ms. Aya Takahashi, Ms. Judith Lermer Crawley, Dr. Victoria Steele, Ms. Deborah Reed, Mr. Masayuki Mochizuki, Mr. Jean-Nöel Grinda, Mr. Ernst Scherz, Ms. Linda Birnbach, Mr. Mark Halpern, Mr. Kiyotaka Fukushima

Chapter 4

Mr. Robert Zwartendijk, Mr. Nathan Lewin

Chapter 5

Mr. Mark Halpern, Ms. Kim Hydorn, Ms. Deborah Remer

Chapter 6

Mr. Hans de Vries, Mr. Ton van Zeeland

Chapter 7

Rabbi Aaron Kotler, Ambassador Kanji Yamanouchi, Mr. Yosuke Watanabe

Chapter 8

Prof. Ewa Palasz-Rutkowska, Dr. Olga Barbasiewicz

Chapter 9

Prof. George Bluman, Prof. Chiharu Inaba

In addition, I am especially grateful to Ms. Harriet P. Schleifer, President of the American Jewish Committee, for contributing the heartfelt foreword to this book.

I am also grateful to a group of French friends of mine who have taken an interest in my research activities and rendered moral support to me during these past years.

Introduction

This year marks exactly ten years since I went to the United States to begin work on my previous book, *Visas of Life and the Epic Journey: How the Sugihara Survivors Reached Japan*, which was published by Kotsu Shimbunsha in June 2012.

On August 29, 2010, I flew out of Narita Airport knowing that I would be able to meet some of the people who were said to have been saved by Sugihara visas. I was excited, but also anxious that I might not get the results I hoped for. In any case, I was determined not to turn back.

The people I interviewed during my three-week trip to Houston, Boston, New York, Washington, DC, and Chicago impressed me strongly, as might be expected of survivors of the unthinkable cruelties of the Holocaust. Fortunately, my book about these people was unexpectedly well received in Japan.

My focus on what happened to the Jewish people who obtained the Sugihara visas and how Japanese people helped their escapes seemed to be why the book was highly reviewed.

With the encouragement of others, I published an English translation of the book in June 2014. This version was accessible to a broader audience. As a result, I have now given more than a dozen lectures in various cities in the United States, Canada, the United Kingdom, the Netherlands, and Lithuania.

In the process, however, a change in my thinking occurred. I had been in awe of the courageous actions of Mr. Chiune Sugihara, but as I continued my research and inquiries, I began to realize that there were other diplomats, both Japanese and foreign, who had worked to save Jews.

It is now said among experts that without the cooperation and goodwill of those people, the escape of these Jews from Europe would not have been possible.

I believe that unless we focus on this point, the story of Mr. Sugihara's "visas for life" will not be properly passed on to future generations.

Objectively speaking, it is undeniable that the way Mr. Sugihara has been portrayed in Japan to date has tended to overly heroize him. Now that international research on Sugihara is progressing, I believe that a broader perspective is necessary.

It would be my great pleasure if this book helps its readers to expand their understanding of the history of the Holocaust.

This book is divided into two main parts: chapters 1 to 3 are sequels to the previous book, and chapters 4 to 8 are introductions to diplomats other than Sugihara who also saved Jewish refugees. In addition, the English version includes an extra chapter summarizing the results of my recent research into details of the Sugihara list—the official list of recipients of transit visas issued by Chiune Sugihara. Because the first half of the book is a sequel, I must warn those who have read my previous book on this topic that some information has been repeated in these chapters.

Akira Kitade

1

Encounter with an Album

Photos of seven faces in an old album … I could never have imagined that an ordinary object would hold so much drama.

It was more than twenty years ago, in May 1998, when I visited my former boss to report that I had returned home after five years of overseas service.

The report was a formality. But there was something else I wanted to discuss. After a perfunctory greeting, I began.

"Mr. Osako, I was surprised to learn that at the beginning of World War II, you were in charge of transporting Jewish refugees who were fleeing Europe to escape Nazi persecution. Could you tell me about that time?"

Mr. Tatsuo Osako joined the Japan Tourist Bureau, the predecessor of today's JTB, in 1938. After the chaotic war and postwar periods, he was transferred to the Japan National Tourist Organization (JNTO) in 1966, at the beginning of the country's rapid economic growth. At the same time, I graduated from university and joined JNTO, and became his subordinate.

Mr. Osako said modestly, "Oh, you mean *that time*. If that's the case, here are some photos from then. Take a look."

What he offered me was an old album.

Most of the photos were in sepia tones. There were five or six pages of meticulously arranged photos of Mr. Osako's time at sea. On one of the pages were photos of seven people's faces. One man, six women. Some showed a lonely expression, some a dark and stern gaze, and one wore a faint smile. Each face seemed to tell a story. The portraits were shockingly moving.

How could they have been preserved for nearly sixty years?

Mr. Osako's story went roughly as follows:

Around the first half of 1940, the Japan Tourist Bureau began to support the escape of European Jews to the United States at the request of an American Jewish organization. The route was to take the Trans-Siberian Railway from Moscow to Vladivostok and go to Tsuruga in Fukui Prefecture on a Japanese ship (the *Amakusa Maru*, 2,346 tons). This long journey was the last escape route left for Jewish refugees because most of Europe had been overrun by Nazi Germany.

Seven photographs taken around 1940

Mr. Osako was assigned the task of conveying the refugees by sea between Vladivostok and Tsuruga. His task continued from the end of 1940 to the spring of 1941, during the harshest time of winter in the Sea of Japan.

Mr. Osako (left) with a female refugee passenger

"The wind and waves were so fierce we were afraid we would sink." Mr. Osako continued, "I don't know how we made it back alive. Most of the passengers on the ship were dressed in shabby clothes and had downcast eyes, giving off the sadness of wandering people who were forced to leave their homeland. I've never been so glad that I was born Japanese as I was then."

The photos of the seven people I had just seen, along with Mr. Osako's story, had a profound effect on me.

In June 2003, five years after our meeting, Mr. Osako passed away at the age of eighty-six. *I should have listened to his story in more detail while he was still in good health.* I felt a deep sense of regret.

Back then, the story of Chiune Sugihara, who is said to have saved as many as 6,000 Jews by issuing visas to pass through Japan, on his own, was gaining popularity here and there. However, the story of how those Jewish refugees arrived in Japan and what happened to them afterward was rarely mentioned.

If this trend continues, the role of the Japan Tourist Bureau at that time will probably be buried in modern history without being known by many people. I heard that most of the Jewish refugees who fled to Japan landed at Tsuruga Port in Fukui Prefecture, where they were warmly welcomed by ordinary citizens, but facts like these will eventually disappear from people's memories. That would be too bad!

I made up my mind to take action. *But where should I start?* The first thing to do was to obtain Osako-san's album, which became the source of my eventual writing.

Mr. Osako's eldest daughter readily agreed. She said, "I would like to thank you for thinking of my father. Please use this album in any way you like."

At the same time, I happened to come across a booklet titled "The Humanitarian Port of Tsuruga" published by the Japan Sea Geographical Survey Research Association. It was a collection of valuable testimonies from citizens who had witnessed Jewish refugees at that time. The booklet was full of information that I needed to know. I immediately contacted Mr. Osamu Inoue, the president of the association.

He said, "I would be delighted to meet you. Please come whenever it is convenient."

The day of my first visit to Tsuruga finally arrived on June 5, 2009. I met Mr. Inoue, an elderly gentleman of small stature, but with a dignified air.

After this visit, my mind was made up.

I will write a book!

In December 2009, I visited the Israeli Embassy and showed the album to the first secretary in charge of public relations, Ms. Michal Tal. I asked for her help in unraveling the mystery of the identity of the seven people in the photos. She said, "I understand your intention. I have only been in Tokyo for a short time, but I feel a strange connection with this amazing story. We will cooperate with the background check of these people."

The young Israeli diplomat's eyes were moist.

Mr. Osako had first showed me the album in 1998. When I borrowed it from his eldest daughter in 2009, it was really a "reunion" with the album after eleven years. After receiving the album, I began to have nightly conversations with these people.

Where in Europe did you escape from? And where did you go after passing through Japan? Are you still well?

On the page I described as "shockingly moving" there were three portraits on the top row and four on the bottom. On the back of each photo, there was a handwritten message. *What does the writing mean?* The messages were in different languages. I had asked the Israeli Embassy to decipher the messages.

The public relations officer, whom I mentioned previously, Ms. Michal Tal, kindly assisted me when I returned to the embassy.

First, in the upper left, the only man. The message in French, beautifully written, expresses his affection for Mr. Osako, "My good memory to my good friend, Tatsuo Osako." I wondered if he had come from France or from French-speaking Belgium. The signature reads "I. Segaloff" and the date is clear: March 4, 1941.

The woman in the center of the upper row. She is breathtakingly beautiful. No wonder Mr. Osako wrote underneath the photo, "She was a woman of unmatched beauty." The message on the back of the photo was written in Norwegian, "To my friend in Japan." I had not expected anyone from Norway. For a woman from a Scandinavian country, Japan must have been a faraway and unknown land. The signature reads "Vera Harrang," but the date is illegible.

Message in French

Message in Norwegian

The woman on the right in the upper row. The message in Bulgarian reads, "To your memory from Henii [her name]." The letters printed on the front indicate that it was taken at a photo studio in the capital city of Sofia. The date reads April 5, 1941. This was around the end of Mr. Osako's term of service aboard the ship.

The woman on the far left in the bottom row, who seemed to be the quietest of the six women, wrote only "Please remember me" in Polish. The message is unsigned, and judging from the inscriptions "40," "X," and "2," the date is most likely October 2, 1940. However, this date may have been the time of her escape from Europe.

Message in Bulgarian

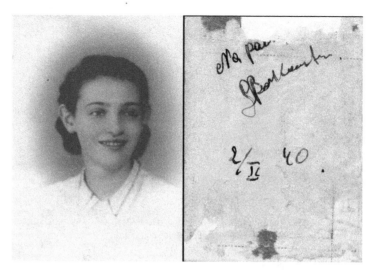

Message in Polish

The woman on her right wrote "Please remember me," also in Polish as in the previous message, but she added the phrase, "To a wonderful Japanese man." To be honest, this woman moved me the most. Perhaps it was the expression on her face that seemed to condense the anguish of the Jews chased by the Nazis. Her signature reads "Rosia," but it is not clear.

The woman on Rosia's right. The message written in French in beautiful handwriting reads, "With all my heart." The signature, "Marie," is also clearly written. Marie has a faint smile on her face. I wonder what she was thinking.

Message in Polish

Message in French

The woman on the right in the bottom row. The message in German is "Dear Mr. Osako, March 22, 1941, on the *Amakusa Maru*." She is the only one of the seven who wrote the name of the *Amakusa Maru*. Perhaps she wanted to say, "Thanks to this ship, we were saved!" It is signed "Toni Altschu. …" It is a pity that the last few letters are missing.

Message in German

As my desire to know what happened to these people grew stronger and stronger, I decided that the only way to write a book was to go out and interview them in person. I finally made up my mind to go to the United States to search for information.

However, going there recklessly surely would not produce results. *What would be the most effective way?*

That's it! The quickest way would be to meet the people who might have landed in Tsuruga on the Amakusa Maru *and ask them to look at the album!*

Then I contacted Tsuruga City Hall and Yaotsu Town Hall in Gifu Prefecture, the birthplace of Chiune Sugihara, for contact information on so-called Sugihara Survivors who were still alive and well. I was fortunately able to get information on nine of them. I had only the addresses for some, for others only their emails, and so on, but I resolved to check them out one by one.

On August 29, 2010, when I took off from Narita Airport, the heat was still intense. My destinations were Houston, Boston, New York, Washington, DC, and Chicago.

On the plane, although I was confident that I would achieve my goals, I was not without a hint of uneasiness. After all, it was seventy years since the people were aboard the ship. Most of the survivors I was about to meet were children when they arrived in Japan. Even if these survivors remembered the seven people in the album, it was highly unlikely that the subjects of the portraits would still be alive and well.

It could end up being a waste of time. I know that. But if I take action, I might be able to get something.

The departure was a mixture of anxiety and anticipation, but there was no turning back now. As I looked down at the scenery around the airport, which was getting smaller and smaller, I made up my mind.

2

The Sugihara Survivors I Met, and the Follow-Up

Mrs. Edith Hamer

Houston, which I visited after twenty-five years, was as humid and hot as Japan. Edith Hamer, a petite woman with beautiful silver hair, who was the first person I was to interview, came to pick me up from my hotel.

"I was three years old when I arrived in the United States via Japan, so I have no memory of that time and I have no idea about the people in the album," she said.

"But a few years later, when I was a little older, my father finished paying back all the money he had borrowed from the Hebrew Immigration Aid Society (HIAS). I can still clearly remember the look of pride on his face.

"Not long after that, my father became ill and died, probably because of all the hard work he had done. My mother remarried. However, her second marriage was not a happy one. Nevertheless, my mother worked hard and gave my younger brother and me a higher education. My heart aches when I think of my parents' less than happy lives. But I think they are happy that we are both living good lives now.

"That's right. It is thanks to Mr. Sugihara that I am now able to live my life in good health. The visa numbers that my parents received from Mr. Sugihara are numbers 7 and 8, and they appear on the first page of the Sugihara list.

"I am ashamed to say that I didn't know until much later that we had been helped by Mr. Sugihara. When I found out, I could hardly wait to express my gratitude somehow. However, it was too late, and Mr. Sugihara had already passed away. Still, I felt I had to do something and decided to write a letter to Mr. Sugihara's wife. It was more than ten years ago now. I wonder if it reached her safely. I heard that she, too, passed away recently.

"The letter? In fact, I have a copy of it here. Please read it if you like."

Mrs. Edith Hamer with beautiful silver hair

I had never expected to be moved in this way at this first meeting with a Sugihara survivor. As I read the copy of the letter that Mrs. Hamer had given me, I couldn't hide my tears in front of someone I had never met before.

Dear Mrs. Sugihara and family,
I do not know how to thank you for giving me the gift of life. However, I think I must do it.
Recently, I learned for the first time about the great deed of your husband, the late Sugihara Chiune, who saved the lives of Jews in Kaunas, Lithuania in the summer of 1940. I was one of the people whose life was saved.
I was a three-year-old child at the time, and my mother put my name in her passport and visa so that I could flee Europe. My parents' visas were issued on July 24, 1940, making them numbers seven and eight on the Sugihara list.
I would like to thank you and your family for the deep compassion, sensitivity, and unparalleled courage your husband showed during this rare and difficult time in world history. It is with the utmost regret that I am unable to express my gratitude directly to your husband. It was nothing but luck that my parents and I were able to meet your husband.
Please accept the gratitude of my now-deceased parents and myself. I am grateful for the opportunity to have survived to this day, to have received a good education, to have lived with a good companion for forty years, to have taught many elementary

school children for twenty-five years, to have raised and educated wonderful twin sons who are now both doctors, to have a granddaughter who is the pearl in my hand, to have friends and an ever-growing family. I am grateful that I have been able to enjoy the company of friends and family that grows each year, and that I have been able to experience the many pleasures that life has to offer.

Unfortunately, I have not been able to find someone to translate this letter into Japanese, but I hope you can understand my intentions.

I have a younger brother who was born in the United States in 1945. My entire family, including my brother, sends our gratitude to the Sugihara family.

We thank you again for the great deeds that Mr. Chiune Sugihara, your husband and the father of your children, demonstrated fifty-seven years ago.

—Edith Finkelstein Hamer, January 23, 1997

It was as if the great impression I had received was "contagious" to Mrs. Hamer. When I couldn't find the right words to say, she looked at me with slightly moistened eyes and concluded her story in a muffled voice, clearly suppressing her emotions. "As Mr. Sugihara saved my life, I will continue to live in good health. So please make sure you come to Houston again."

Mrs. Hamer's hand was warm and full of compassion. I said goodbye, confident that I would be able to see her again, as she was still in her early seventies.

Since Our Interview

When the English version of my previous book was published, as mentioned in the Introduction, I sent the completed book to the people I had interviewed, and Mrs. Hamer was the first to reply. The warm atmosphere at the time of our parting was conveyed directly in her email of appreciation.

Two years later, in April 2016, I called Mrs. Hamer at her home in Houston. I was going to participate in a Japanese government-sponsored event related to Chiune Sugihara in Los Angeles in June, and I wanted to ask her if she were interested in joining me in the event as a Sugihara survivor. Normally I would have emailed her, but I had a hunch. The person who answered the phone was her husband.

"Hello, yes, this is Hamer. Kitade from Tokyo? Sure, I remember you well. I read your book with great interest."

"Thank you for remembering me. Is Edith at home?"

"Edith … My dear wife … She passed away last February. She was sick."

"Oh, I don't know what to say."

"If she had been well, she would have gladly gone to Los Angeles. It's a shame. We used to talk about you a lot. There still is a copy of your book on her desk. She was incredibly grateful to you."

I couldn't come up with the right words in English, so I hung up the phone without being able to say anything more. In fact, I had been visiting the United States every year since 2012. Most of my visits were to the East Coast, mainly to New York. Each time, I thought of visiting Houston, but due to various restrictions, I could not make it. I greatly regretted that.

Before publishing this book, I wanted to remember Mrs. Hamer, so I asked her husband to send me some of her recent photos. They were all of her later years and she looked happy. One of them was with her granddaughter, Sonia. Sonia made a trip in July 2017 to trace her grandmother's escape from the Holocaust and Mr. Hamer sent me her account of the trip. If Mrs. Hamer were still alive, she would have been delighted to see how her grandchildren have grown up. For twenty-five years, as an elementary school teacher, she had taught children, through her own experiences, how dangerous human hatred, prejudice, and indifference can be.

In each place she visited during her trip, Sonia must have been thinking about the lessons her grandmother left for her.

Mr. and Mrs. Hamer, who loved each other

Mr. Samuil Manski

Samuil Manski, who was waiting for me at a nursing home in the suburbs of Boston, was so familiar that I could not believe that we had never met before. This was because I had seen him many times in the Fukui TV documentary, *After the Door Opened*. However, I couldn't deny that he looked very haggard.

"I'm actually suffering from cancer right now," he said. "But I'm not afraid of dying at all. I not only survived but was blessed to have a family. I have three sons, two of whom are university professors, and one who is an executive at a bank. I will be ninety years old next month. Thanks to Mr. Sugihara, I have been able to live this long, and I am fully happy.

"About these people in this album? Well, it was seventy years ago, and our family was confined to our cabin on the bottom deck of the ship. I don't even remember if the ship was called the *Amakusa Maru* or not. What I do remember is that when the ship left Soviet territorial waters, there was a huge cheer, and everyone went on deck and started singing what is now Israel's national anthem, 'Hatikvah.'

"After that, we landed in Tsuruga, which was heaven for us. The town was clean, and the people were polite and kind. We even got to eat bananas and apples. Eating bananas was especially a new experience for me.

"Now I have nothing left to regret. There are people like you who come all the way from Japan to see me … I may not see you again, but I wish you good luck in your current endeavors."

Mr. Manski followed me to the entrance of the nursing home and did not move from his spot until my cab had departed. When I turned around in the back seat, he was still standing under the blazing sun in the same place, watching me drive away. His composed appearance showed the strength of a man who had survived the Holocaust.

Mr. Manski, who said, "Now I have nothing left to regret"

Since Our Interview

On June 23, 2011, the Japanese newspapers simultaneously reported the following short news item: "Samuil Manski, one of more than 6,000 Jews saved by a visa issued by Japanese diplomat Chiune Sugihara to pass through Japan during World War II, died Sunday at a hospital in Hyannis, MA, friends and the Consulate General of Japan in Boston revealed. He was ninety years old. He was known for his efforts in raising funds to build a monument in honor of Chiune Sugihara."

On the day I visited Mr. Manski at the nursing home, I met his wife as well. But she was not in good spirits at that time, and after exchanging brief greetings, she left without joining our conversation. I later learned that she passed away in March of the following year.

I had no contact with the Manski family after Mr. Manski's death, and I was unable to deliver the English version of my book to them.

Five and a half years after Mr. Manski's death, in December 2016, Mr. Manski's nephew, Mr. David Manski (I will call him David from now on), contacted me. His father was Mr. Manski's brother. David approached me, asking for my advice on a trip he and his wife Shira were planning to take from August to September in 2017 to retrace the escape route of his father's group in 1941. The group of refugees had consisted of Mr. Manski, his sister, his brother (David's father), and their mother.

David and Shira's journey was to begin in Poland, the family's homeland. They would fly from Boston (they lived in Bar Harbor, Maine) to Warsaw, then to Lida (now in Belarus), the hometown of their father and his family, to Kaunas, Lithuania, where the group temporarily took refuge (and where they obtained their Sugihara visas), to Moscow, the starting point of the Trans-Siberian Railway, to Vladivostok, the final train stop, and from there to Sakaiminato by sea. (Ships no longer sail from Vladivostok to Tsuruga.) They would stay in Osaka for a week. During this time, they would visit Kobe, Tsuruga, Yaotsu Town, and finally they would come to Tokyo and return home from Narita.

I met them in Tokyo on September 16, 2017 as we had arranged in advance, and we visited Yokohama at my suggestion. There we went to see the NYK Maritime Museum and the *Hikawa Maru*, which was moored in Yamashita Park. David was deeply moved by the *Hikawa Maru*, which is said to be the same type of ship as the *Hie Maru* that his father and his family boarded. On the ship, we toured the cabins from first to third classes. David's words, "My father and his family would not have been able to stay in first class," were filled with his heartfelt feelings for his family and showed his warm and rich humanity.

David and Shira Manski, at the NYK Maritime Museum

The photo shown here is of the three children of the Manski family, taken during the Jewish New Year in 1931: Mr. Manski (eleven years old at the time) on the right; his younger sister, Mira (nine years old then), on the left; and his younger brother, Saul (David's father, three years old in the photo), in the center. It was eight years before the German invasion of Poland, and you can see that it was still a peaceful time.

The Manski children during peaceful times

Mr. Manski's eldest son, Charles, is a professor of economics at Northwestern University in Chicago and was nominated for the Nobel Prize in Economic Sciences in 2015. During my interview with Mr. Manski, I told him that I would be stopping in Chicago, and he said that he would be happy if I would meet his son. I tried to make an appointment with Charles, but unfortunately it was not possible because he was on a business trip the day I was scheduled to visit Chicago.

When David heard about my efforts to reach out to his cousin, he said he would tell him about it when he got back to the States. I never expected to receive an email from Charles. However, sometime after David went back home to the United States, I was thrilled to receive this message from Charles:

> Dear Mr. Kitade,
> My cousin David recently told me that you would like to correspond, and he gave me your email address. I am glad that he did. I had wanted to write to you earlier, to let you know how much I enjoyed and learned from your book.
> Unfortunately, I was unable to find your email address on my own.
> I obtained a copy of your book and read it some time ago, and I now have looked at it again. You have performed an important service by calling attention to and documenting the vital role that the JTB played, including Mr. Osako, in making it possible for the refugees to reach Tsuruga. Of course, Mr. Sugihara deserves enormous thanks for initiating the process that enabled the refugees to survive. Nevertheless, there is often an understandable tendency to personalize history too much, focusing attention on one great man and forgetting the contributions of others. Your book reminds us that many people helped to make the journey possible.
> While reading your book, I was surprised and moved to find the part where you recall meeting my father in Framingham in 2010, including your photo with him. I had been aware that my father had contacts with various people from Japan. However, I had not known that you had visited him personally. The period when you met, in September 2010, was not easy for him. My mother, whom you may have met as well, was declining into dementia at that time. This weighed heavily on my father. As I think you know, they both died in the first part of 2011, first my

mother in March and then my father in June. Of course, they both had lived very long and mostly happy lives, so there are no regrets. Indeed, it seems miraculous that my father, who could so easily have died in Europe during the war, was able to live to age 90 in Boston.

Although my father had talked often about his journey and wrote about it in his book, I feel that I did not really understand much of it until 2009, when I visited Kyoto for a conference. On that visit, two former Northwestern PhD students with whom I remain friends, Tsunao Okamura and Emiko Usui, accompanied me by train to Tsuruga to visit the museum there. Tsunao and Emiko, who are married, had learned about Sugihara while in school in Japan, so they were interested to make the trip. They are both economics professors, Tsunao at Yokohama University and Emiko at Hitotsubashi University. Later on, in 2011, my son Ben and his wife Sarah visited Tsuruga as well.

David tells me that you are in process of writing a sequel to your book. I look forward to seeing it when it becomes available.

Regards,

Charles Manski

Because of the interviews I conducted seven years before, I was later able to meet such wonderful people as David and Charles. I think that this good fortune was brought about their father, Mr. Manski.

Prof. Charles Manski

Mrs. Lilly Singer

She was a truly cheerful and lively old lady. Both Mrs. Hamer and Mr. Manski, whom I met earlier, gave me a sense of melancholy that came from their having fought to overcome their harsh fates before finally achieving happiness.

Mrs. Singer however, seemed to say, "Harsh fate? I have nothing to do with such a thing." She also had a great sense of humor.

As soon as we greeted each other, I took out my Osako album and began asking the questions.

"Of these seven, these two seem to be from Poland, and the message on the endorsement appears to be in Polish. Can you read this one?"

"Honey, I was born and raised in Poland. Let me look at it. Well, this letter looks hard to read. *Please remember me ... to a wonderful Japanese ...* That sounds like it."

"When I first saw these photos, I was wondering what kinds of feelings these people had when they handed their pictures to Mr. Osako. If that's what this message means, then it must have been given out of gratitude for all the help she received while on board, right?"

"Probably so. But I think your boss might have requested it. They are young girls, you know."

I didn't know how to respond.

"Just kidding. By the way, what's the purpose of your doing all this research?"

"I want people to know that there were people behind the scenes who supported Mr. Sugihara's great humanitarian deed, and I plan to write a book about it."

"That's great! I would love to read it. So, when will the book be ready?"

"I've just started my research activities. I'm going to publish in Japanese first and I'm not sure when I'll be able to publish it in English."

"That's too bad."

"I'm sorry. I'm not a professional writer. By the way, would you like to say something as a Sugihara survivor?"

"I have a lot of feelings about Mr. Sugihara. As you know, the Israeli government gave him the title of 'Righteous Among the Nations' in 1985. In fact, I'd wanted to write a letter to thank him even before then, but I wasn't able to do it. So, I thought it would be a good opportunity to write one, and I did. But then, I heard that Mr. Sugihara was gravely ill. I felt really embarrassed at my negligence. There is nothing more painful than writing a letter to someone when you knew he is very sick. I wrote to thank him belatedly for saving my life and to express my sympathy for his illness, but I couldn't fully express my feelings. I still feel bad about that. More importantly, I wonder if Mr. Sugihara read my letter.

"I pray that you will be able to find the whereabouts of the people you are looking for. And don't forget to publish your book in English."

It had been with a twinge of sadness that I said goodbye to Mr. Manski, but I didn't have to deal with such a melancholy feeling with this gutsy woman.

At this rate, this lady will be fine for a long time.

Instead of feeling being pulled back, as I had when leaving Mr. Manski, I left as if I were being strongly pushed forward.

Lilly Singer, saying, "I was born and raised in Poland"

Since Our Interview

After the 2010 interview, I published the Japanese and English editions of the book in two-year intervals and maintained some form of contact with the people I had interviewed and their families.

Unfortunately, I lost contact with Mrs. Singer after I sent her the English version. As I mentioned above, I had several opportunities to visit New York afterwards, so I wanted to visit Mrs. Singer in her suburban New York home to ask her what she thought of the English version that she had been so concerned about. I was also hoping that I might be able to hear her dry comments full of her characteristic humor.

However, I heard that she had lost her beloved daughter at that time and was very depressed. I spoke with Kuniko Katz about this. It was Kuniko Katz who had brought me to Mrs. Singer in the first place. She also helped me with the translation of the English version, and she is the person to whom I owe the most. We decided to leave Mrs. Singer in peace, and meanwhile several years passed.

When I was writing the manuscript for this book, I was curious about Mrs. Singer, so I casually searched for "Lilly Singer" on the Internet. To my surprise, I found a YouTube clip of Mrs. Singer appearing on a TV station somewhere in the United States and giving an interview.

The program was about Chiune Sugihara. It was a stage play performed by an Australian actor of Japanese descent. Mrs. Singer appeared as a Sugihara survivor in the play. The play was a cliché, but the fact that a Sugihara survivor herself was commenting on it seemed to have some impact.

The program was aired on November 11, 2014, and I wondered if it was before or after the loss of her daughter. Either way, I can only hope that she is still in good health. (Translator's note: Mrs. Singer passed away before the Japanese version of this book was published.)

Dr. Sylvia Smoller

Dr. Sylvia Smoller greeted me smilingly in a room of her ultra-luxury apartment in the center of Manhattan, New York. She is known as the person who donated to the town of Yaotsu in Gifu Prefecture a passport stamped with the Sugihara visa that saved her life and the lives of her parents. Most of the Sugihara survivors who received the request for the donation from Yaotsu Town said, "Please forgive us for refusing. It's our family's lives." It is said that Dr. Smoller was the only one among them who willingly agreed.

Dr. Sylvia Smoller, who was waiting for me with home-cooked food

I asked her to look at the Osako album, which was the purpose of my visit.

"You took the trouble to bring these precious photos from Japan," she said. "Unfortunately, I have no idea who any of them are. But what a handsome man Mr. Osako was. If I had been a young girl, I would have fallen in love with him."

Perhaps seeing me looking discouraged, she tried to soothe my mind by making a light joke.

In turn, she showed me a picture. To my surprise, it was a picture taken in front of Kiyomizu Temple where they traveled to Kyoto during their stay in Kobe. Even though they were refugees, the people in the photo were all dressed in fine clothes. I heard that Dr. Smoller's father was an official in the Polish Ministry of the Interior, and the highest-ranking Jewish official in the government.

There was something I had really been wanting to ask Dr. Smoller. It was of course about the passport that was donated to Yaotsu Town. It must have taken a great deal of determination to make that decision, but where did that generosity come from? When I mentioned it, she nodded with a smile and offered me a piece of paper.

"It was on December 4, 1993, that the passport presentation ceremony was held in Yaotsu. At that time, I was asked to give a speech. Here is the manuscript. Please read it later if you like."

The visit was so enjoyable that I regretted leaving. I was told many valuable stories and appreciated her unexpected hospitality, including homemade food. As soon as I got back to my hotel room, I read through the manuscript of her speech to soak in the afterglow.

An excerpt of the speech follows.

> It is my great pleasure to present you with this passport today. This is a testament to the humanitarian spirit of Chiune Sugihara, a man whose noble deeds saved thousands of lives.
> In the Talmud, the holy book of Jewish law and tradition, there is a saying, 'He who saves one life saves the world.' I would like to say to all of you that Mr. Chiune Sugihara is the one who played the role of "saving the world."
> When I was a child, my parents and I came to Lithuania from Poland to escape the persecution of the Nazis during World War II. To escape Europe, we needed a visa to enter a third country. Jews who could not leave Europe were certain to die in Nazi camps. There, they were sent to gas chambers and their bodies were burned in incinerators.

The consul in Lithuania, Chiune Sugihara, was an outstanding and honorable man who understood the position of the refugees and could not help but extend a helping hand to them. So, he helped them by issuing them transit visas to Japan. Without permission from his home country, he issued thousands of visas for life, bearing the red official seal of Japan. We are among the 6,000 people who were able to come to Japan because of his visa and were saved by it. The reason I am standing here today is because Mr. Chiune Sugihara saved my life … .

I would like to express my deepest gratitude for the favor I received in 1940 and for the favor you have shown me today in 1993.

That visa saved the lives of three members of the Hafftka family.

Reading her speech brought back all the emotions I had felt when I was shown the passport photos at Dr. Smoller's house just a few hours before. The passport was unmistakably stamped with "Consulate of the Empire of Japan in Kaunas" and contained a visa handwritten by Chiune Sugihara.

Passport stamped with the Sugihara visa

At the passport presentation ceremony, held in 1993 at Yaotsu. Photograph provided by Yaotsu Town

Since Our Interview

After the interview in 2010, I had many opportunities to meet Dr. Smoller, in contrast to Mrs. Hamer, Mr. Manski, and Mrs. Singer, whom I never met again.

I hope you will forgive me for going off on a tangent here.

In September 2014, I was fortunate to be invited by the Daiwa Anglo-Japanese Foundation in London to give a lecture to its members. About seventy percent of the participants were local British people and the remaining thirty percent were Japanese people living in London. One of them was an up-and-coming filmmaker (director and actor) who introduced himself as Junichi Kajioka. Kajioka-san (as I called him) was the first to approach me at the reception after the lecture. He offered to make a documentary on my pursuit of the seven members of the Osako album. The conversation proceeded at a brisk pace.

Two months later, in November, Kajioka-san flew in from London to coincide with my visit to New York. I introduced him to Dr. Smoller and he shot film while interviewing her.

Dr. Smoller, who appeared in the finished Kajioka film (entitled *Sugihara Survivors: Jewish and Japanese, Past and Future*), referred to the English version of my book.

"I had always thought that there must have been other people besides Sugihara who helped those Jewish refugees, and Kitade's book helped me to understand that. I think he did a really good thing by writing about it."

It is still fresh in our memory that the movie *Persona Non Grata (Chiune Sugihara)* was released to the public on December 5, 2015. About a week before that, the producer from the Nippon Television Network who created the movie asked me to introduce a Sugihara survivor I knew. He said he was looking for someone who would appear on stage to give a speech at the opening of the film in Tokyo. I recommended Dr. Smoller without hesitation. I thought we would have a reunion in Tokyo, but it turned out to be quite the opposite, because I was scheduled to go to New York just then. A few days after the opening, however, Dr. Smoller returned to the United States. At her home in Manhattan, showing no signs of fatigue, she told me in detail what had happened at the opening.

I met her most recently on August 4, 2017, during the annual Sugihara Week organized by Yaotsu Town. At this time, the town organized a lecture by Dr. Smoller, and Kajioka-san and I were invited as co-participants.

First, a documentary on Kajioka-san's work was screened, and he talked about the background of its production in a witty manner. As I mentioned earlier, this documentary followed my activities, so I frequently appeared in it. I felt slightly embarrassed to watch the film with the audience in the packed hall.

Next, I gave a talk entitled "My Encounter with Dr. Smoller," in which I shared my story of our first meeting in 2010.

At the end of our talks, Dr. Smoller, with a stately gait, appeared on the stage, dressed beautifully, with a big smile on her face. It was as if her aura radiated and the atmosphere in the hall seemed to have changed drastically.

She is far more than a match for us! I muttered in my mind.

The lecture, which began in a quiet tone, soon stirred up excitement in the hall in response to the enormous scale of its topic.

> Have you ever heard of the 'butterfly effect'? It is said that the flap of a butterfly's wings causes the air around it to vibrate, which eventually spreads throughout the world and ultimately causes climate change. That is the butterfly effect.
> At that time, many Jewish refugees were saved thanks to the visas issued by Consul Chiune Sugihara in Kaunas, Lithuania. Among them, there were talented scholars, scientists, artists, musicians, politicians, and doctors. Now, their descendants are working all over the world.

Mrs. Masha Leon

Masha Leon when she was younger

"I'd like to invite you to my house, but I'm working on the interior. So, let's meet at my favorite restaurant instead."

The next day, I met Masha Leon at the designated Chinese restaurant, and she seemed unexpectedly much younger than I had imagined.

"This was the starting point of my Holocaust experience," she began.

"After the German invasion of Poland in September 1939, my mother and I fled Warsaw. At that time, a farmer gave us a ride in his wagon. He said he would take us to the suburbs. The cart was already full of about twelve people. The farmer collected all the valuables from us. He said that even if the Germans found them, he would not be searched. He took us to the German headquarters and said, 'I've brought you a group of Jews,' and took our belongings away.

"We were made to line up against the wall of the building, and the Germans put a number tag on each of us. Then we were made to stand all through a long winter night. At dawn, the German soldiers came back with pistols in their hands. Then the shooting scene that is often seen in movies unfolded. It was the odd-numbered people who were killed. My mother and I were separated from each other, and luckily, we both had even numbers, so we miraculously survived. It was up to the whims of the German soldiers at the time to decide whether the numbers should be odd or even."

In these peaceful times in the free and glamorous city of New York, I was overwhelmed by the stories that I had only known from movies or read about. I didn't know how to react to a person who had actually experienced such unimaginable events. Masha-san (I addressed her with that name) continued, ignoring my perplexity.

"Then there was the opposite case …

"Germany tried to drive the Jews out of German territory, and the Soviet Union wouldn't let them into Soviet territory, so the people stuck on the border collapsed from hunger and cold. We were trying to rely on my mother's parents, who lived in Soviet territory. I had the mumps and was running a fever. At that time, a farm woman came to our rescue. She hid us in a wagon and brought us safely out of German territory. She then hid us in her barn for a while. It was at a time when the whole village would have been executed if it were discovered that they had helped Jews.

"My mother offered her some money to thank her, but the farmer wouldn't take it. 'I am a Christian and it is my responsibility to help those in need. If I take the money, I will no longer be a Christian.'

"Oh, no, I'm the only one talking. I'll have to hear your story, too. Oh, yes, it was about the *Amakusa Maru*, wasn't it? The sea was very rough, and the ship was rocking a lot. Everyone was seasick and vomiting all over the place. As a result, the cabin was filled with an offensive smell. It was so bad that I went out on the deck and played by myself. For some reason, I didn't mind the rocking of the ship. I remember one of the crew told me that the children should go down below.

"Oh, this is Mr. Osako? I don't remember him because of the situation. Unfortunately, I have no idea who these seven people are, either. Besides, they may not have been on the *Amakusa Maru* at the same time as us.

"By the way, I heard that you will be meeting Leo (referring to Mr. Leo Melamed, mentioned later) in Chicago, please give him my regards."

"Pardon?"

I was about to put my food in my mouth when my hand stopped.

"Oh, you didn't know? Leo and I have known each other since we were little. Both of our families lived in Vilna for a time before we fled Europe. At that time, there was a birthday party for me, and I have a picture of us all together. This is the picture. There are fifteen or sixteen children in this picture, but most of them were sent to concentration camps and lost their lives."

I was quite surprised to learn that Masha-san and Mr. Leo Melamed had known each other for a long time. What a surprise to find that both were in the limited group of nine I had planned to interview!

I would have liked to have continued the interview, but Masha-san, an active journalist, was busy with another appointment.

At Masha's birthday party. Right side, fifth from front is Masha. Left front is Leo Melamed. The picture was provided by Masha Leon

"I'm sorry we didn't have enough time, but if you have any questions, please feel free to email me. And be sure to let me know the next time you're coming to New York," Masha-san said, and walked out of the restaurant as briskly as she had entered.

Since Our Interview

In my previous book, it was essential to write about Kobe, the last stop for many of the Jewish refugees who arrived in Japan. On the morning of March 7, 2012, before I left home for Kobe, I checked my email and found a message from Masha-san in New York.

"I'm sending you a photo I found of a park I walked in during our stay in Kobe. Unfortunately, there is no record of the name of this park. At that time, we refugees were not allowed to carry cameras around. Someone from the Japanese group that took this photo sent it to us where we were staying, and this is the only photo we have of us in Japan."

Hinda Oler   Zelda Bernstein   Masha Bernstein   Hannah Oler

A rare picture showing refugees with Kobe citizens

I had planned to go to Kobe in the hope of finding something that would show the traces of interaction between Jewish refugees and ordinary citizens, but to my surprise, the "proof" came to me before I left. While I was on the Shinkansen, a Japanese bullet train, I was captivated by the photo, and glad that Masha-san was concerned that I had not done enough research in New York.

After that, I continued to keep in touch with Masha-san, and she also agreed to be interviewed by Junichi Kajioka, for the aforementioned documentary.

The following year, on April 27, 2015, when Prime Minister Abe visited the Holocaust Museum in Washington, DC, Masha-san and Leo Melamed each shook hands with him as representatives of the Sugihara survivors.

On April 5, 2017, when I thought she was still in good health, I received an email with the subject line "Sad News."

"Akira-san, I have sad news. This morning, my mother passed away in her sleep. Thank you for your kindness and friendship until now. Just a quick note to let you know.—Karen."

Karen is Masha-san's second daughter, and we had met several times before. I conveyed the news of her death to Yaotsu Town, Tsuruga City, and Fukui TV. A few days later, I received another email from Karen.

"Akira-san, I can't thank you enough for what you have done for my mother. The many emails we received from Japan were a great comfort to us. You have been a true friend to my mother. She always looked forward to hearing from you. You have enriched my mother's life. I hope you will continue to do so. Japan, Tsuruga, Kobe, and the heroic act of Chiune Sugihara occupied a large part of my mother's heart.

Domo arigato gozaimasu.—Karen."

In this way, another valuable witness to the Holocaust, or rather, a friend whom I'd found through the mysterious workings of fate, had left this world.

Mr. Benjamin Fishoff

"Take a look. This is my entire family. Five children, twenty-six grandchildren, and great-grandchildren … how many?"

Benjamin Fishoff, an eighty-seven-year-old still active as a banker, proudly showed me a large photo of his family. I showed him the photos from the Osako album.

Fishoff family group picture. Photograph provided by Mr. Benjamin Fishoff

"Let me see. These people were on board *Amakusa Maru*, did you say? Well, I don't have any idea about them. In fact, I had a very difficult time on the *Amakusa Maru*. I will never forget that day. It was March 13, 1941. As soon as our ship arrived at Tsuruga, the immigration officer came on board to check our passports. He told us that we would not be allowed to enter the country because we did not have visas for the next destination country. We desperately pleaded with him that we would arrange the necessary documents through the mediation of the Kobe Jewish Association, but we, seventy-four altogether, were sent back to Vladivostok on the 16th, three days later.

"This time, Soviet officials called us 'spies for Japan' and we were confined to the ship for several days. In the end, we headed back to Tsuruga with no prospects, but as we approached the port, we saw someone we recognized waving at us. It was a person from the Kobe Jewish Association. Thanks to the efforts of the Association, we were finally able to land in Japan. March 23 was the day I should call 'my fateful day.'

"The Kobe Jewish Association negotiated with the Dutch Embassy in Japan and obtained a certificate for us to land in Curaçao. You know about Curaçao, don't you? To explain briefly, we could go to the island of Curaçao, at that time a Dutch territory in the Caribbean, without a visa, but we needed a document to prove it. So, before we left Lithuania, we refugees went to the Dutch Consulate in Kaunas, but it was already closed by Soviet decree. Therefore, we came to Japan with only a Japanese transit visa that was issued by Mr. Sugihara at the Japanese Consulate, and that is how we ended up in such a situation. Anyway, as it turned out, we were able to enter Japan.

"By the way, I will change the subject a little bit, but I had dinner with Mr. Zwartendijk's three children here in New York a few years ago. Mr. Zwartendijk was the Dutch consul in Kaunas at that time, and like Mr. Sugihara, he was the one who issued certificates of entry to Curaçao (commonly known as Curaçao visas) to many of our compatriots. [Author's note: See chapter 4.] In other words, like Mr. Sugihara, he is a benefactor for us Jewish refugees. So, the Jews in New York who were saved by the Curaçao visa gathered and held a welcome party for Mr. Zwartendijk's children.

"I thanked them at the dinner and asked them how they knew who I was, even though it was decades ago. They gave me a surprising answer. The National Archives in Washington, DC has a list of seventy-four names. I still wonder how a list prepared by the Dutch Embassy in Tokyo ended up in the National Archives.

"In any case, I was able to reach Japan thanks to Mr. Sugihara and Mr. Zwartendijk. However, for various reasons, I could not leave Japan immediately and stayed in Kobe until August 1941, when I was deported and sent to Shanghai. Finally, in 1947, I was able to come to the United States all alone. My parents and siblings stayed in Europe, and they were all killed later."

Each Sugihara survivor may have had a different fate, but Mr. Fishoff's story seems to have been particularly tumultuous.

By the way, I must confess that I did not know much about the "Curaçao visa" mentioned in Mr. Fishoff's story at that time. However, I became deeply involved in the issue a few years later, for reasons that I will describe in detail in chapter 4.

Since Our Interview

Mr. Fishoff in his office

I met with Mr. Fishoff several times in New York afterwards. To be specific, I had many difficulties regarding the publication of the English version of my book, and I consulted with him. Since the book would be read mainly in the United States, I tried to find an American publisher. In order to do so, I had to prepare an English manuscript. I asked three acquaintances living in New York to share the translation. This cost me a significant sum. Of course, this was out of my own pocket. However, it was not easy to find a publisher who would accept the book. Self-publishing was an option, but the translation fee would have exhausted my funds. In the meantime, Mr. Fishoff had been generously providing me with helpful advice. But when I asked him about raising funds for self-publishing, he instantly turned into a pragmatic banker, all business.

In the end, I was fortunate enough to get a Japanese publisher to accept my proposal, and after more than two years of struggling, the English version finally saw the light of day. When I sent the finished book to the people concerned, I received a phone call from Kuniko Katz. She had also helped me with the translation. She said, "Yesterday, I received a call from Mr. Fishoff telling me that the book had arrived. He was very happy and wants to send you a check as a gift to congratulate and thank you. He would like to know your address."

For a moment, I couldn't understand what was going on. As soon as I finally understood, I started to cringe. Perhaps Mr. Fishoff was concerned that he had not been able to help me with my publication in the United States.

A few days later, I was surprised when I saw an airmail envelope in my mailbox. It was flimsy. When I tried to open it, I found that about a quarter of the seal was open. I opened it, my heart pounding with worry. Sure enough, there was a check inside, but no written message addressed to me, nothing.

I was lost in thought. Would a check of this amount be nothing more than a piece of paper to Mr. Fishoff? No, not at all. I guess it is his aesthetic sense to send a check without any formalities.

That night, I sent a polite thank-you email in the Japanese style. His reply was simply, "My pleasure."

No superfluous words, just the necessary words. This is Mr. Fishoff's style. Still, I felt that he had put a lot of his feelings into those two words.

Like Dr. Sylvia Smoller and Mrs. Masha Leon, two other Sugihara survivors described above, Mr. Fishoff also cooperated with Kajioka-san in the making of his documentary. With the Sugihara list in hand, Mr. Fishoff was eloquent.

"This is the last page of the Sugihara list. My name is at the top. My name is number 2070. The last number is 2139, so I was one of the very last people on the list. You can see how lucky I was."

NR.	NATIONALITY	NAME	ENTRANCE OR TRANSIT	DATE OF VISA	SASHOOMIO PIKOO
2070	Polish	Chil Benjamimn Piszof	TRANSIT	21/VIII	2
2071	"	Heres Bregman	"	"	2
2072	"	Maria Aslanowicz	"	"	2
2073	"	Jan Michalski	"	"	2
2074	"	Janusz Zambrowicz	"	"	2
2075	"	Zambrowicz Maja	"	"	2
2076	Lithuanien	Swirska Sonia	"	"	2
2077	Polish	Ehrlich Irja	"	"	2
2078	"	Honigsberg Zelik	"	"	2
2079	"	Szyfer Wanda	"	"	2
2080	"	Honigsberg Rajzla	"	"	2
2081	"	Szyfer Jerzy	"	"	2
2082	Tchecoslov.	Leblova Mariana	"	"	2
2083	Polish	Sokonska Majka	"	"	2
2084	"	Morenshildt Sergiusz	" "	"	2
2085	"	Szkornik Zofja	"	"	2
2086	Lithuanien	Mangejm Sara	"	"	2
2087	"	Bela Jonas	"	"	2
2088	Polish	Szapiro Salomon	"	"	2
2089	"	Rymer Mojżesz	"	"	2
2090	"	Dreszerowa Anna	"	"	2
2091	"	Lewin Srul	"	"	2
2092	"	Sadowski Izrael	"	"	2
2093	"	Haftka Hela	"	"	2
2094	"	Baumgatten Necha	"	"	2
2095	"	Wulfson Hersz	"	"	2
2096	"	Frydman Izrael	"	"	2
	"	Rakowicka Miriam			2

Sugihara list showing Mr. Fishoff's number was 2070

Mr. Jan Krukowski

It was finally time for my last interview in New York. I left the hotel with a lot of time to spare so that I wouldn't be late for my appointment, but I still got caught in a traffic jam. Seeing me in a hurry, the cab driver graciously lent me his cell phone.

"I'm fine," Mr. Krukowski said. "Please take your time and don't panic."
He sounded kind.

Mr. Jan Krukowski, who said, "My father trusted the Japanese emperor"

In the end, I was fifteen minutes late. In spite of this, the Krukowskis greeted me with smiles. The interview began in their living room with its wonderful view overlooking the East River.

"When we left the territorial waters of the Soviet Union, almost all the passengers went on deck and began singing, in unison, 'Hatikvah,' which later became Israel's national anthem. It was truly an explosion of joy. My father, who was standing beside me, put his hand on my shoulder and said, 'It's all right now. From now on, the Emperor of Japan will protect us.' Hearing this, I suddenly felt closer to Japan, which I had never known anything about before, and I realized how great the Emperor really was.

"We were really worried until we arrived in Vladivostok and boarded the ship. Before we arrived there, we had purchased regular train tickets in Moscow from Intourist in dollars. The Soviets wanted dollars very badly, so we were treated as ordinary travelers, not refugees, and the crew was relatively friendly. However, the Trans-Siberian Railway was single track and we had to stop frequently to let oncoming trains through. In the end, it took us two weeks to get there. After such a tedious train ride, we were elated when we got on the ship. So even though it was old and smelly, and we had to sleep on the floor, we felt no pain at all.

"However, my sister developed a fever, so when we landed in Tsuruga, we decided to stay there. I don't know how my father found it, but we decided to stay at a Japanese inn. There was a brazier in the middle of the tatami room, and a fire was burning. It was the first time in a long time that we were able to sleep in a warm room in a house. That's right. That was our first night in the land of the free.

"But there was something different about that memorable night. There were a lot of women in kimonos and heavy makeup, clearly different from the inn's employees. We could hear the sound of musical instruments and laughter. There were quite a few men coming and going, who looked like customers. Apparently, it was … "

And there Mr. Krukowski smiled wryly.

"It was a brothel, wasn't it?" I asked.

At this point, I used the word "brothel" instead of "geisha house" for *yukaku*, revealing my poor vocabulary.

Then Mrs. Krukowski, who was sitting with her husband, burst out laughing and turned to him and said, "That's a house of ill repute, right?"

I had never heard that phrase before, so I couldn't comprehend what it meant right away.

"In other words, it means that the house had a bad reputation."

I see. "A house of ill repute." Indeed, it was the perfect phrase to describe yukaku.

I felt a little embarrassed. The word "brothel" generally means "a house of prostitution" and it lacks the atmosphere of *yukaku*. I had an unexpected English lesson.

"You had a precious experience so early in your life."

I was enchanted by Mrs. Krukowski's typically American dry sense of humor.

I heard with surprise that she was a professional singer who had performed at the Twenty-Fifth Tsukuba International Music Festival held in 2009, under the name of Nancy Harrow. She had studied classical piano from age seven through university. She had gone to Paris where she sang in such places as the Mars Club. It was no wonder that she was always smiling and had the mannerisms of a true entertainer.

The combination of someone who had lived in such a glamorous world and someone who had suffered as a refugee seemed incongruous to me. However, Mr. Krukowski's hardship occurred a long time ago. I felt that it was not right for me to feel that way.

As I was about to leave, I offered them a coaster set of ukiyo-e woodblock prints that I had brought as a small souvenir and said, "If I ever come back to visit you again and you offer me tea, please use these."

It was a very brazen thing for me to say, but Mr. and Mrs. Krukowski were happy to accept such words.

Since Our Interview

To tell you the truth, I was remiss in showing my gratitude to the Krukowskis. Although I had been to New York many times since then, I had not visited them even once. However, I unexpectedly stumbled upon a chance to make up for that ingratitude.

In June 2017, when I gave my second lecture in London, I had a chat with a Japanese woman, Keiko (a pseudonym), who came to listen to me. She had something interesting to say.

"I have an American friend who is a musician, and he told me that his father was helped by the Sugihara visa. His name is Damon Krukowski."

Could it be?

I returned to the hotel, suppressing my excitement, and when I entered the room, the first thing I did was open my computer.

I typed in "Damon Krukowski," and sure enough, several photos appeared. When I saw the face of the man holding a guitar, I was convinced that he looked exactly like the Mr. Krukowski I had met seven years ago. I immediately called Keiko to tell her what I had found out.

Sometime after my return to Japan, I received an email from her.

"Damon and his wife, Naomi, are going to Japan soon for a concert. This is their schedule for your reference."

I visited Damon at a live music club in Shibuya one evening in November, when pleasant autumn weather was in the air.

"I met your parents in New York in September 2010. I've written about it in this book, so you can read it later."

Damon was very pleased with my unexpected visit, and we agreed to meet again in a few days to discuss more. On the morning of November 13, I met him at a coffee shop near the hotel where he was staying, as he was returning to the United States on a night flight.

"I read your book with great interest last night. I was very surprised to read so many things about my father that I didn't know. My father was eleven years old at the time, so he must have remembered a lot.

"Yes, my grandfather's name was Edward, number 296 on the Sugihara list. My grandmother? Yes, her name was Alice, and her number was 258 on the Sugihara list. I don't know why the numbers are so far apart, but my grandmother was also a registered visa holder. Polish names end with an 'i' for men and an 'a' for women. Therefore, my grandmother's last name was Krukowska. My father and aunt were children, so I assume they were covered by my grandfather's visa."

Thanks to Damon's explanation, what I had only vaguely understood before became clear.

At that moment, his wife, Naomi, arrived late. She explained that she had been shopping for souvenirs. She also performed with Damon as a singer. Damon plays acoustic guitar, and Naomi plays electronic piano and sings. Naomi's performance a few days before, singing songs with lyrics in both English and Japanese, had been very impressive.

It was hard to leave the couple, but I couldn't keep them too long before they left for the airport.

"The next time you come to Japan, let's make time to talk. Please give my best to your father and mother."

Damon and his wife, Naomi, who performed memorably in Tokyo

Mr. Rick Salomon

The Salomon family. Far left is Mark. Photograph provided by Mr. Rick Salomon

There is a town called Skokie, located about a thirty-minute drive north of Chicago.

In 2007, a new Holocaust Museum opened there. The official name of the museum is the Illinois Holocaust Museum and Education Center.

On September 13, the day after I traveled from Washington, DC to Chicago, I visited the museum and met with Rick Salomon, who had been very helpful to me during my trip to the United States.

This is how it happened.

In February of the same year (2010), an article about the Osako album that I had received from the Israeli Embassy was published in *Yedioth Ahronoth*, a major daily newspaper in Israel. Mr. Salomon, who saw the article, sent me an email.

"My father was one of the Sugihara survivors who came to the United States via Vladivostok and Tsuruga and I was born after that. Judging from the newspaper articles, I believe that my father was also on the *Amakusa Maru*. I heard that there is still a logbook written by the crew, can you show it to me?"

It seemed that Mr. Osako's recollections were reported as the logbook. I explained this to him, and he sent me another email.

"I went to Tokyo last March and visited the Foreign Ministry's Diplomatic Archives and was shown the Sugihara list where my father's name definitely appeared. The issue number was 299. The purpose of my visit to the Archives was to request the loan of materials related to Mr. Sugihara to be displayed in the newly opened Holocaust Museum. As a member of the preparatory committee, I have been working hard for many years to collect materials related to Sugihara. Please find an opportunity to visit our museum in the near future."

Because of this exchange, there was a familiarity that made it hard to believe we were meeting for the first time, and the conversation was lively. We knew that he was in a position that had nothing to do with the seven members of the Osako album, so we exchanged opinions and information from a different perspective.

There has always been a Jewish community in the town of Skokie, and in 1997, a neo-Nazi group applied for an antisemitic march there. The village filed a lawsuit to prohibit the march. However, the Nazi group, represented by the American Civil Liberties Union, filed a countersuit to allow the demonstration. After more than a year, the Supreme Court held that under the Constitution's First Amendment right to freedom of speech, the Nazi group had the right to march.

Mr. Salomon explained to me that although the Nazi group won the suit, they decided not to march in Skokie. It was against this background that this museum was established, and I was reminded of the depth of antisemitic sentiment.

When we parted, Mr. Salomon presented me with a wonderful gift.

"This is an essay written by my college student son, Mark, which won an award. You can read it if you like."

It's a little long, but I share an excerpt of this piece.

The Gift of Life

By Mark Salomon

To save one life is to save humanity.—Talmud

My life began on March 24, 1989, but my story begins fifty years earlier in in war-torn Poland with the border closed and encircled by Nazi storm troops. Passed down from generation to generation, my ancestors' stories became part of my own. The main characters are my grandfather, a Polish Jew and Holocaust survivor named Bernard Salomon, and Chiune Sugihara, a Japanese diplomat with absolutely no connection to my family. While my grandfather's life path was a modern-day odyssey, it was the actions of Mr. Sugihara that would influence me in unimaginable ways. At a time when so many turned their backs on the atrocities surrounding them, the Japanese consul to Lithuania did the unthinkable simply by listening to his conscience.

After unsuccessfully attempting to transfer his parents to safety after the Nazi invasion, my grandfather was forced to travel alone, by foot, over barbed-wire terrain on a 170-mile journey from Mlava, Poland to Kaunas, Lithuania. Bernard did not have much of a chance to share his story and passed away in 1955, when my father was less than two years old.

As the situation for the refugees became even more desperate, Sugihara met a delegation, including my grandfather's brother, at the embassy in Kaunas. Looking into the gathering sea of faces, Sugihara took a morally courageous stand and at great risk to his family and himself, he provided the 299th exit visa to my grandfather on July 30, 1940 ... to permit safe passage by train through Siberia and by boat to Kobe, Japan. My grandfather then traveled to Shanghai and then to Calcutta, India.

In all, Sugihara issued 2,139 visas for Jews to escape the Holocaust. If not for his actions, my grandfather would have died in a concentration camp, and my Dad, my sister, and I would not be here either. With later generations, Sugihara is said to have saved over 300,000 lives. As a result of his actions, his diplomatic career was ruined and at a one point, he was penniless on the streets of Tokyo.

How did Sugihara's actions affect me? He taught me that unjust laws must sometimes be broken, and discriminatory public policies must be actively fought, for justice to prevail. He demonstrated that one person truly can make a difference. No act of racial or ethnic hatred can be countenanced; indeed, no act is too small or insignificant to be ignored. Whether it is on the playground where a bully taunts another student, in the classroom where disrespect or insensitivity is directed to a learning-disabled child, or on the sport field where an epithet is hurled against the member of racial minority, each of us must fight on a daily basis the urge to be a bystander. We must take a stand, ever harkening back to the universal lessons of the Holocaust, to fight hatred in all its forms, to teach the insidious consequences of prejudice, and to nurture an understanding that differences among peoples, far from being feared, should be fostered… .

This essay is the result of the lessons of one life saved by Chiune Sugihara being passed on to the next, and the next, and the next. The grandson of a Sugihara survivor is touched by his father's story of the hardships his own father endured.

Since Our Interview

To my surprise, this essay took an unexpected turn. In June 2017, I received a call from the Aichi Prefectural Board of Education. The purpose of the call was as follows.

"Next year, Aichi Prefecture will hold a ceremony to commemorate Chiune Sugihara at his alma mater, the former Aichi Prefectural Fifth Middle School, now Zuiryo High School, in Nagoya. We are planning to display the text of Mark Salomon's essay in one corner of the facility. We would like to ask you to act as an intermediary."

I immediately approached his father, Rick Salomon, who was delighted to get Mark's approval, and he agreed to work directly with the school board.

Preparations progressed steadily, and the unveiling ceremony was to be held on October 12. The school board wanted to invite Mark to the ceremony, but he was on his honeymoon and would not be able to attend. It was a disappointment for both parties.

But what a wonderful thing to start a new life on the same day that the story of his grandfather, who gave him life, was to be announced far away in Nagoya, Japan.

Rick Salomon, a devoted father, informed me that Mark is a member of a law firm in New York. He handles complex commercial disputes such as breach of contract and securities fraud, as well as class action lawsuits, and is a promising young lawyer.

This is one of the results of the "butterfly effect" that Sylvia Smoller told us about.

The memorial to commemorate Chiune Sugihara at Zuiryo High School in Nagoya.
Photograph provided by the Aichi Board of Education

Mr. Leo Melamed

The amiable Mr. Leo Melamed

It was finally time for my last interview. The man I was going to meet was the "father of the financial futures market" and one of the most powerful people in America. I had been told by someone who knew the situation that "he is a big shot, and rarely agrees to meet people." However, I think it is human nature that makes you want to meet a person like that even more.

That's right, the Israeli Embassy in Tokyo! I realized I could ask for their help in arranging an interview.

"Mr. Melamed responded. He said he would be happy to meet with you. He will be waiting for you in his office at 3:15 p.m. on September 14th."

This email from Michal Tal, Secretary of the Israeli Embassy, jumped out at me. It is often said, "One will take a chance because one has nothing to lose," and that's exactly what I did. Even so, "3:15" seemed to indicate a minute-by-minute schedule, and I was immediately wrapped in a sense of tension.

Now, the day of the event.

I carefully arrived at my destination by 2:30, and after taking a good breath in the lobby, I stood in front of the receptionist a little after 3:00. At 3:15, the appointed time, the secretary came out and asked me to wait a little longer. I waited for about fifteen minutes and then the man himself appeared, saying, "Thank you very much for waiting."

I was prepared to be overwhelmed by intimidation, but I felt a little let down. The big name who is said to be running the financial world in the United States had now reached the age of *kiju* in the Japanese sense of the word, the enlightened state of mind associated with reaching the age of seventy-seven. Standing before me, Mr. Melamed seemed more like a good-natured elderly gentleman.

"Masha called me from New York and told me about her meeting with you. Yes, she and I were childhood friends.

"By the way, I heard that the purpose of your visit to the United States was to look for people related to the *Amakusa Maru* that we were on.

"Let's see, these are the photos of those people…. Well, I have no idea who they are. Anyway, it was pitch black when we boarded the ship. We were crammed into a huge room on the bottom floor with no bed or mattress, and because it was so cold, my mother held me tightly as I slept.

"However, the sea was very rough, and the ship was rocking heavily. Most of the people went up to the deck with buckets in their hands. Even so, the stench filled the room, and it was unbearable.

"Anyway, thanks to that ship, we were able to escape safely to Japan. If I go back further, it was thanks to Mr. Sugihara's visa, after all. And we were saved by the country of Japan. And now that I've heard your story, I've learned for the first time that we was also helped by a Japanese travel agency. It seems that your old boss, oh, yes, that Osako-san, also helped us, and I am sincerely grateful to him.

"As our *Amakusa Maru* approached Tsuruga Port, the snow-covered surrounding mountains loomed before us, a beautiful sight indeed. I felt very warm even though it was winter. No wonder. We had come from Siberia, where it was extremely cold, dozens of degrees below zero.

"When we landed, the town of Tsuruga looked like a miniature garden. Most of the houses were made of wood, and inside the houses, you could see doors that looked like they were made of paper. The people wore straw hats and seemed to be shoveling snow. My impression of the people was that they were very simple and seemed to be kind. The language I heard was from another world, and I felt like I was really in a foreign country.

"From there, we went to Kobe. We stayed there for about four months, so I have many memories of Kobe. But to tell you the truth, our stay in Kobe was not a relaxing one. It was an urgent one for our family. We did not have a visa to enter the United States. We heard that the US Embassy in Tokyo was a better place to apply for a visa than the US Consulate General in Kobe, so my father made frequent trips to Tokyo. He was still worried about it, so he and a friend rented an apartment in Tokyo and went on a pilgrimage to the embassy. It must have been difficult for my father to live a double life in Kobe and Tokyo.

"In the end, we were able to manage to get a visa just in time and left the port of Yokohama in early April of 1941. The ship we boarded was a large freighter called the *Heian Maru*, which was a world of difference from the *Amakusa Maru*.

"The two-week voyage on the Pacific Ocean was comfortable. After all, there was no need to worry about eating. This was a blessing for a child in the prime of his eating years. On the way, I met a boy around my age, and we became good chess buddies. He was from India and spoke Hindi, and I spoke Polish and Yiddish, and even though we didn't speak each other's language, our hearts communicated very well with each other."

I was drawn into Mr. Melamed's story as if I were listening to a tale of adventure on a grand scale, but I became concerned about the passage of time. When I looked at my watch, I realized that the hands were already pointing to 4:30. I had been told by the secretary that I had about thirty minutes scheduled for my interview.

As a sign that it was time to wrap up, I said what I had thought of saying beforehand.

"My efforts began with a desire to shine a spotlight on the people who quietly supported Chiune Sugihara's great humanitarian deeds in a world where wealth and fame were not part of the equation. I want the people of the Jewish community to know that."

Mr. Melamed's last words were the best encouragement for me as he spoke politely and calmly in spite of my halting English.

"I agree with you. Thank you for coming all the way from Japan."

On April 3, 2011, Jiji Press reported that Mr. Melamed had sent a message of encouragement at the time of the Great East Japan Earthquake, saying, "I am confident that Japan will overcome the current hardship."

Since Our Interview

When I was struggling to publish the English version of my previous book, I received a call from an acquaintance.

He said, "I just came back from the United States yesterday. When I met Mr. Melamed in Chicago, he was worried about what happened to the English version of your book. He told me that he had an idea about the publisher, so why don't you contact his secretary?"

That Mr. Melamed!

I was so thrilled that my heart was filled with excitement. I immediately sent an email to his secretary, who emailed me back to inform me of the person in charge at a certain publishing company in New York. Without a moment's delay, I sent the English translation to the person in charge.

"I read your manuscript, but I regret to inform you that our company specializes in economics, so we are unable to meet your request."

Of course, I am not a world-famous writer like Haruki Murakami …

After many twists and turns, the book was published in English in Japan in June 2014 by Chobunsha under the title *Visas of Life and the Epic Journey*.

It was around this time that I received the news of Mr. Melamed's visit to Japan.

On July 1, he gave a speech at the Foreign Correspondents' Club of Japan. I was also invited to the luncheon and was able to meet him again after four years. It was fortunate that I was able to hand over the English version of the book, as it had just been completed.

In fact, that day, July 1, 2014, was a critical day that could determine the fate of Japan in the future. The government held an extraordinary cabinet meeting to approve the exercise of the right of collective self-defense. Just before the extraordinary cabinet meeting, Mr. Melamed paid a visit to Prime Minister Abe at the Prime Minister's Office. The Prime Minister's Office may have wanted to reschedule the visit, but the fact that the prime minister accepted the visit as scheduled shows the extent of Melamed's influence.

During his visit to Japan, Mr. Melamed visited Tsuruga, which was his first "homecoming" in seventy-three years. Fukui TV made a documentary on the visit, and I wonder how Mr. Melamed must have felt as he stood in front of Tsuruga Port, where the *Amakusa Maru* arrived seventy-three years ago.

Three years later, in November 2017, Mr. Melamed received the Order of the Rising Sun from the Japanese government at the fall awards ceremony.

As the Sugihara survivors I interviewed are leaving us one by one, I can't help but hope that Mr. Melamed, who turned eighty-eight this year, will continue to be active and healthy for many years to come.

Mr. Leo Melamed, receiving the award of the Order of the Rising Sun from the Japanese government

3

People in the Album Whose Identities Were Discovered

Part 1

Sonia

"Kitade-san, one of the seven people has been identified!"

On April 8, 2014, my eyes were glued to an email sent by Ms. Aya Takahashi, who lives near Vancouver, Canada. She is a journalist who has been following up on Sugihara survivors living in Canada, and she is a comrade of mine, so to speak.

She has an acquaintance, a female photographer living in Montreal. The photographer's name is Judith Lermer Crawley. Her parents are Jews from Poland, who were also helped by Sugihara visas.

Judith's mother was the eldest of five sisters. She was pregnant when she fled from Poland to Lithuania, so her sister Zosia accompanied her. For some reason, Zosia got separated from her sister and her brother-in-law and came to Japan later. Fortunately, Zosia was able to obtain an American visa and finally arrived in the land of the free.

Now, in February of 2014, Judith had happened to find a photo of the seven people in the Osako album on the website of Yad Vashem, Israel's official Holocaust remembrance organization. The photo was the one I had provided through the Israeli Embassy in Japan several years ago, requesting them to release the information.

When Judith saw the photo of one of the seven, she intuitively thought, "This must be my aunt!" When she informed her cousin Deborah (Zosia's eldest daughter) in New York, Deborah said, "It's definitely my mother!" It was that woman, second from the left on the bottom row of the Osako album, who I remember moved me the most when I saw her photo for the first time.

It had been sixteen years since Mr. Osako had shown me the album, five years since I started research for my book, and, more than that, seventy-three years had passed since Mr. Osako had been handed the photo by the woman on the run.

Immediately, Deborah and I began exchanging emails, and I learned the following.

Deborah's mother's name, which seemed to read "Rosia," was actually "Zosia." Zosia Gertler was born on November 5, 1923 in Lodz, Poland. She landed in Tsuruga, Fukui Prefecture in early 1941, and left Yokohama on April 10, on the *Yahata Maru* of the NYK Line.

At that time, after reaching the United States through an arduous journey of escape, Jewish refugees often took new names to live by in their new land. Zosia became Sonia in America. She married Curt Reed, another Jewish refugee, in June 1946. Sonia Reed had her first daughter Deborah in September 1951, her son David in May 1954, and her second daughter Shelley in December 1958.

After her life became stable, she and her husband visited Japan twice, and the latter half of her life was happy. Sonia Reed passed away on September 8, 1997 at the age of seventy-four.

Sonia's two other children also confirmed that the photo was their mother's. Afterward, Deborah provided me the following information on behalf of her siblings.

> Our parents initially lived in New York City, where our mother learned to sew and speak English while working in the garment industry. For the next few years, they ran a small clothing store. After the birth of their first child, they moved to the suburbs on Long Island where our father began working as a sheet metal fabricator. Our mother helped him run the factory. Because of her work, she became an enamel artist and was a lover of art,

music, and theater. As Jews, our parents were committed to Jewish education and had many friends and close contact with their relatives in the United States, Canada, Israel and Mexico.

Our parents' business was small, but they invested mainly in Japanese products and seemed to be quite successful. They traveled to Japan twice and loved Japanese culture.

Throughout her life, our mother was heartbroken by the loss of her family in the war [World War II], but she never talked about it with us in detail.

The three of us were very surprised and excited when we were informed about the existence of her photo. We are grateful for the people who conducted this research. At the same time, we'd like to express our gratitude to let us know the existence of these humanitarian people who saved our mother and many other refugees.

When we saw the photo, we immediately recognized our mother and were moved beyond words. We know very little about her life at that time, but we feel that this photo helps us remember what it was like.

My younger brother and sister remember that our mother never talked about her escape trip from Europe, but I was told that she was treated very kindly by the Japanese.

I couldn't help but think that there was some mysterious force at work in this series of events, and I began to think that the photo should be returned to the children. I looked for an opportunity to do it, of course, with the consent of Mr. Osako's eldest daughter.

Fortunately, the opportunity came surprisingly quickly. On November 24, 2014, seven months after the news of Zosia's identification, the Consulate General of Japan in New York kindly held a grand ceremony at its official residence to return the photo. Deborah's younger siblings and their families, as well as her cousin Judith, who came from Montreal with her daughter, attended the ceremony. It was a reminder of how important family ties are to Jewish people.

"Our mother's message to Mr. Osako was, 'Please remember me.' Her wish was fulfilled. Not only was she able to survive, but she was certainly remembered. At the same time, she also remembered the kindness of the Japanese people toward our countrymen in their time of need."

Deborah's acknowledgement moved the audience to tears.

With Sonia's three children

It was as if I were watching a great drama, and I was immersed in the afterglow of emotion for a while, because the identity of a person was revealed after more than seventy years. It is human nature to get greedy, and I began to wonder if I could find one or two more people.

And then it became a reality. In 2015, the seventieth anniversary of the end of World War II, the world was filled with talk of that great conflict. As if in response to this, one person was identified in July, another in August, and two more in September. I couldn't believe it.

Part 2

Antonina

The next person to be identified was a woman who left a message in German in the album. Her official name turned out to be Antonina Altszuler. She was born in 1919 in the town of Kalwaria Zebrzydowska in southern Poland. After landing in Tsuruga, she moved from Kobe to Shanghai and finally came to the United States in 1949. She married and changed her name to Antonina Babb. However, her husband died a few years later. She eventually moved to California and worked as a librarian at the University of California, Los Angeles (UCLA) for thirty-eight years before passing away in 1994 at the age of seventy-five. At that time, she donated her estate of $600,000 to the library. As she had no children, she had no one to take care of her toward the end of her life, and the details of her last years are still unknown.

Sonia, described in part one, was blessed with a good family and lived a happy later life, but I could not help feeling that Antonina's life was somehow covered with a shadow of misfortune.

In June 2016, on a visit to Los Angeles, I visited the UCLA library. The wonderful silver-haired director, Dr. Vicki Steele, greeted me smilingly. To my surprise, she said, "I used to work at the library with Antonina for a short time. At your request, I searched for photos and documents from those days, but unfortunately, I couldn't find anything. She was a bit nonconforming. She spoke like a man and had masculine mannerisms. She didn't get along with her coworkers and was always alone."

The day before, I had made contact with the only woman Antonina had been close to in her later years. I had asked to meet her, but she refused, citing old age. However, the woman told me the location of Antonina's cemetery. Unfortunately, it was impossible for me to go there myself, as I was scheduled to return to Japan the next day.

"Oh, you have information about Antonina's cemetery? Well, I'll ask someone to go there later to take pictures."

Vicki was sympathetic toward my lack of success, and she was kind enough to help me.

A few days after I returned to Japan, I received an email from her. "I went to the cemetery yesterday on my own to take a picture, so I'm attaching it here. It was a Christian cemetery called Holy Cross, and her headstone had a cross carved on it. I wondered why she was buried as a Christian when she was Jewish. As you can see from the photo, some parts of her tombstones were missing, and it looked like the grave had not been taken care of. I guess not many people had visited this place."

Antonina spent the first half of her life in hardship, fleeing persecution, and the second half of her life in solitude without a single relative.

In March 1941, she had handed Mr. Osako a photograph of herself on board the *Amakusa Maru* with the words, "Dear Mr. Osako." This may have been one of the few times in her life when she felt hope and happiness.

Visiting UCLA library with Vicki Steele (top); Antonina's tombstone, photograph by Dr. Steele (bottom)

Part 3

Next up to be identified was a Bulgarian-speaking woman. From the Cyrillic letters printed on the surface of the photo, which indicated "Sofia," I had guessed correctly that she was from Bulgaria. Fortunately, I found out that her eldest daughter was living in the United States, so I contacted her immediately.

However, the daughter said, "I don't mind, but my brother and sister want me to never disclose anything about our mother. They insist that if any information becomes public, they will be hurt. I'm sorry that we can't comply with your wishes, but please understand."

I had assumed that they would be pleased, as in the case of Sonia, and I felt as if cold water had been thrown on my head. However, when I thought about it calmly, I realized that all people have wounds in their hearts that they don't want others to touch.

As I was reflecting on the fact that I had been too self-complacent, I received a big package from the eldest daughter. When I opened it, I found three paperback books and two somewhat old hardcover books. The first paperback book was written by the eldest daughter and described her involvement in various social activities. The other paperbacks also related to her activities. The two hardcover books were written by her mother, the woman in the photo. The contents were a record of her struggle with an incurable disease.

I had a rough idea of their situation.

A few weeks later, I met that daughter for the first time in New York. To see me, she and her husband took turns driving from the town in Michigan where they lived. We met at a restaurant in Brooklyn called Shalom Japan. It was an appropriate place for a Jewish couple and me, a Japanese, to have dinner.

Thanks to the thoughtfulness of the eldest daughter of the woman in the Osaka album, I gained another unforgettable experience in my "epic journey" of searching for people.

Part 4

Nicky, formerly Nissim

Now, it was time to meet the only man in the photo album.

From the beautiful French message on the back of his photo, I thought he was from a French-speaking country, but he was also from Bulgaria. He was born in 1896, which means that he is the only one of the seven people in the album who was born in the nineteenth century. On February 1, 1941, in Sofia, he obtained a visa to immigrate to the United States and landed in Tsuruga on March 4 on the *Amakusa Maru* with Mr. Osako on board. He then arrived in Seattle on March 16 aboard the *Hie Maru* of the NYK Line from Yokohama. This itinerary clearly shows that he was not a Sugihara survivor. His original name was "Nissim Segaloff," but he changed it to "Nicholas Sargent" after moving to the United States.

Sports Illustrated, a leading American sports magazine, reported that he was a world-famous backgammon player. Although he did not win the first international backgammon tournament held on the island of Grand Bahama in 1964, it is reported that he survived to the end. Curiously, his whereabouts after that notable achievement are unknown. In combination with the fact that he changed his name as mentioned above, there is something mysterious about him. Since he was said to have been fluent in French and English, there were rumors that he might have been a CIA agent.

Subsequent research, however, revealed that the following article appeared in the British weekly magazine *The Spectator* on January 27, 1979.

> Born just before the turn of the century in a town halfway between Bulgaria and Serbia, Nicholas Sargent (former name, Segalov) is said to be the first backgammon hustler. After taking money from Mr. Guggenheim (a member of the Guggenheim family) in Europe, he boarded the *Titanic* with him. Mr. Guggenheim went down with the ship, but Mr. Sargent survived. He is still a hustler at the prestigious Palace Hotel in Gstaad, but he seems to have lost his way lately with the rise of younger players.

At first reading, I was astonished that he was a survivor of the *Titanic* incident. I couldn't believe it. He was born in 1896 and would have been sixteen years old when he sailed on the *Titanic* in 1912. But it's not impossible.

I immediately checked the *Titanic*'s passenger list on the Internet. I found the name of "GUGGENHEIM, Mr. Benjamin" among the first-class passengers. Benjamin was the fifth son of Meyer Guggenheim, the founder of the Guggenheim conglomerate. Benjamin Guggenheim is known as one of the most prominent passengers who shared the fate of the *Titanic*.

Next, I checked the name "Segaloff." I couldn't find it among the first-class passengers, or even among the second- or third-class passengers. Continuing my search, I found another list dedicated to "survivors." With my heart pounding in my chest, I proceeded to check, but until the very end, I didn't come across any names that looked like that.

Of course! Even if he were really on board, it was unlikely that he would have used normal means to get on the ship. He probably used a fake name. The article in the weekly magazine said, "he took money from one of the Guggenheims." Perhaps he was invited by Guggenheim to play a game with him during the voyage ...

I was drawn into the world of my imagination.

In the meantime, there was a small development.

It was March 2016, and the setting was Union Square in the center of Manhattan, New York. It is a place where I often go for a walk as it is very close to my regular lodgings when I'm in town. On that day, I met a group of people playing backgammon in a corner of the square. I don't know anything about the game itself, but I was curious about it in relation to Segaloff, so I decided to take a look.

"Can you play the game?"

"No, I'm just interested ..." I explained about my search for a particular player.

"Are you Japanese?"

"Yes, I am, but ..."

"So, do you know Mochii? You don't? He's a Japanese world champion. We're backgammon players, so we know each other well. I'll tell him about you. Why don't you ask him about Nicholas Sargent? My name's Junior."

I was skeptical. Junior told me that Mochii was spelled "Mochy," so I typed in "Mochy backgammon" to see if I could find anything on the Internet about a world champion. Sure enough, there it was! Mochy seems to be quite a figure in the world of backgammon.

In June, I received an email from Mochy, which I did not expect at all.

"Hello. My name is Masayuki Mochizuki, and I am a professional backgammon player. The other day, I got a call from my friend Junior in New York ..."

The polite tone of the letter made me cringe. In fact, I should have contacted him first myself. I wrote back immediately and sent him a copy of my book so that he would understand the situation.

Two years passed without any progress. I guess this is why the proverb says, "Good things come to those who wait."

"Hello. This is Mochizuki. You contacted me in 2016. I reread the book you sent me and tried to find out if anyone knew Nicholas Sargent, and I got some useful information.

"I would like to introduce you to a man named Jean-Noël Grinda and ask you to contact him. He was the world backgammon champion in 1997 and a great tennis player who represented France at the Davis Cup in the 1950s. I heard that he once played backgammon with Nicholas Sargent. He is a close friend of mine, so I will contact him."

I immediately sent an email to the address that Mr. Mochizuki had given me and received a brief but favorable reply from Mr. Grinda.

"The information you sent enabled me to find out that there were a number of things I didn't know about Nicky. [Author's note: Nicky was Nicholas Sargent's nickname; I'll call him that from now on.] In particular, I was surprised to learn that he was born in 1896. In his later years, he was in and out of the Palace Hotel in Gstaad, and it seemed that he was very alert. I'm sure there's something else I can tell you, so give me a call if you like."

I dialed the number at the specified time, and Mr. Grinda answered immediately. Since the call followed the exchange of emails, there was no need to introduce myself. Mr. Mochizuki had told me that Mr. Grinda lived half in the United States and half in Europe. His phone number seemed to be in Europe, so I asked him where he was staying. To my surprise, he said he was in Gstaad, Switzerland—where Nicky had stayed in his later years! I thought that it was impossible, but when I asked if he was at the Palace Hotel, he said yes. I believed it was a fateful coincidence, but it was probably only me who thought that. Mr. Grinda must have been staying there for a long time. And this hotel may have been the place where they communicated.

Jean-Noël Grinda (legendary tennis player)

Mr. Grinda told me the following story about Nicky.

"That's right. It was at the Palace Hotel that I first met Nicky. I think it was in 1973 or 1974. One day, I saw an old man standing in the lobby of the hotel. He seemed to be looking for a partner for a game of backgammon.

"The game started, and I watched from the side, but his manners were not good. He didn't try to hide his frustrated attitude, and he used foul language. His bets were $5 or $10 at most. That's how he earned small amounts of money, little by little, playing with beginners. But he was very good at it.

Palace Hotel, which Nicky frequented

"I would ask him to play with me from time to time, but more often than not, I would watch him play games with others. I learned the game that way. In that sense, he was my teacher. However, I never paid him to teach me. He never wanted to take money from me.

"One winter night I was driving my car and Nicky was walking in front of me. Apparently, he was on his way back to his apartment. The road was icy, he was unsteady on his feet, and he caught his foot on the ice and fell. It was hard for him to get up. I stopped my car. A car behind me tried to pass. I felt that Nicky was in danger, so I jumped out of my car and helped him up. He looked quite injured. I tried to take him to the hospital, but he stubbornly resisted.

"I persuaded him to go to the hospital and get treatment. I knew he had no money, so I tried to pay for his treatment, but he refused. He was such a proud man.

"What happened to him after that? I don't know the details, but I heard that he died in Cannes in the south of France. All his personal belongings were said to be deposited with the concierge of the Carlton Hotel there, but I don't know if that's true."

Mr. Grinda's story conjures up an image of the despondent figure of Nicholas Sargent, once one of the best backgammon players in the world.

I should mention that on March 5, 2019, I visited the Palace Hotel, which Nicky is said to have frequented as a backgammon hustler in his later years. It is one of the leading hotels in Gstaad, a high-class resort in Switzerland: very dignified. I arranged in advance to meet Ernst Scherz, the former owner of the hotel, who welcomed me warmly.

"I actually saw Nicky, who used to come and go here," he said, "but that's the extent of my contact with him. When I heard that you were coming today, I asked someone special to come and meet you."

Just as I was wondering who it was, the person appeared.

"I'd like to introduce you to Mr. Taki Theodoracopulos, the writer who interviewed Nicky at the time. I'm sure it's difficult for newcomers to remember his name, so Mr. Taki will do."

I was taken aback by this unexpected turn of events. I remembered the name Taki. It was he who had written the article about Nicky in the British weekly magazine, *The Spectator.*

"I remember the first time I met Nicky in Paris in the 1970s …

"Oh, you mean the *Titanic* incident? He told me about it, and I might have dramatized the story a little … No, it was over forty years ago, so I've forgotten the details."

Depending on how things went, I might even have gone to the Carlton Hotel in Cannes, but after hearing Mr. Taki's "confession," I lost all interest.

My visit to the Palace Hotel taught me the lesson of moderation in curiosity.

Mr. Scherz (former owner of Palace Hotel) on the left. Mr. Taki on the right

Part 5

Vera

The last of the five people whose identities were discovered in a chain reaction was a person who deserved to be the "finale." It was that beautiful Norwegian woman. Fortunately, I was able to contact her eldest daughter, Linda, who lives in a suburb of New York.

She said, "What a wonderful cause you are working on. I would like to tell you everything I know about my mother, so please feel free to ask me anything."

The response was more positive than I had expected, and I decided to take the plunge and fly to New York in December to visit Linda.

To my surprise, the Norwegian woman named Vera Harang was not Jewish. When Mr. Osako first showed me the album, I had assumed that the seven people in the album were all Jews because of the association with Chiune Sugihara.

So why did she have to flee Europe?

The victims of the Holocaust were persecuted by the Nazis and sent to concentration camps to die because they were Jews, but I was unknowingly unaware that there were many people who fell victim to the inhumane policies of the Nazis despite not being Jewish.

Vera was one of those rare victims who escaped the Nazis by the skin of her teeth. As a young woman, she had worked for the Norwegian Red Cross. She was well known for her good looks. At the time, Ingrid Bergman was already a famous actress, and there were those who suggested that Vera, who was almost as good-looking as Bergman, should enter the film industry. However, this idea was dropped when Norway was invaded by Germany in April 1940.

Vera, working at the Norwegian Red Cross. She is third from the right

As a patriot, Vera tried to join an underground organization to resist the Germans. At that time, young women were being kidnapped frequently in Norway. Vera's mother, fearing for her daughter's safety, decided to let her go to the United States.

Another inhumane policy of the Nazis was called the Lebensborn (Fount of Life) Program. They abducted young blonde and blue-eyed females and forced them to have children fathered by SS soldiers because blonde hair and blue eyes were considered indicative traits of superior races. Then the babies were taken in by childless SS families and raised as Germans. There were many Lebensborn institutions in Norway that took temporary care of such babies.

One of the Lebensborn institutions

As I listened to the story of Vera, who narrowly escaped the clutches of the Nazis thanks to her mother's courageous and wise decision, and who went on to live a full life in the United States via Tsuruga, Japan, I strongly felt that fact is stranger than fiction.

The story of the Lebensborn Program was particularly shocking.

I would like to continue with the story of Vera, who was lucky not to become one of its victims.

According to Linda, Vera was born in the town of Drammen, Norway in 1917, the youngest of six siblings. Her father ran a general store but passed away when she was a child. In 1940, she was working for the Red Cross, but after the German invasion of Norway in April, she tried to join the resistance movement. However, at that time, there were frequent abductions of young women by the German SS in the country. As mentioned above, a courageous mother decided to let her daughter escape to the United States.

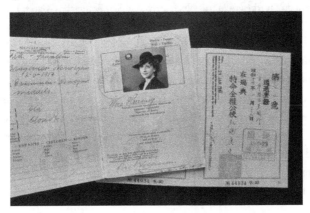

Vera's passport

Following the suggestion of her mother, who was from Sweden, Vera went to the United States Embassy in Stockholm on February 1, 1941, to obtain an immigrant visa. Three days later, on February 4, she went to the Japanese Embassy to obtain a transit visa, and then to the Soviet Consulate to receive another transit visa. On February 10, she registered for a two-day stay in Moscow with the Moscow Labor and Peasant Police. She then took the Trans-Siberian Railway and boarded the *Amakusa Maru*, where Mr. Osako was on duty, in Vladivostok. Crossing the harsh Japan Sea in midwinter, she landed in Tsuruga, Fukui Prefecture, on February 23. On March 6, she departed Yokohama aboard the *Tatsuta Maru* of the NYK Line and arrived in San Francisco on March 20. The fact that she reached her destination only forty-eight days after obtaining her US immigrant visa suggests that her escape was very carefully planned.

Vera on the *Tatsuta Maru*, which arrived in San Francisco (March 1941)

What is even more astonishing is it usually took about two weeks to complete the Trans-Siberian Railway journey in those times, but in Vera's case, it took only ten days. And the trip between Vladivostok and Tsuruga took three days and two nights under normal circumstances. I'm amazed that she was able to travel from Moscow to Vladivostok to Tsuruga in a little less than two weeks. Just following the itinerary of the flight is a harrowing experience. This background seems to convey the desperate prayers of a mother for the safety of her daughter.

What happened to Vera after she arrived in the United States, the land of freedom?

In 1942, she married Emil Kronberg, a Jewish man from Austria. In 1946, she visited Norway. In 1949, she gave birth to Linda and in 1951, she visited Norway again with Linda. In 1974, Mr. Emil died at age seventy-two. Linda says that Emil loved Vera, who was fifteen years younger than he, all his life. Vera never visited her homeland a third time. She had been a modest person until the end.

When I said, "If Vera had entered the film industry back then, I'm sure she would have become a popular actress in Hollywood," Linda's answer was, "Well, I don't know." Like her mother, she was modest. After I returned to Japan, I received an email from Linda.

"I didn't have enough time to talk to you the other day. To tell you the truth, my house burned down in a fire in 1985. During the fire, my mother ran into the bedroom on the second floor and escaped with only a small box that she had always cherished. Most of our household goods were lost. The only things left in the box were the few old photos I showed you the other day and my parents' passports.

"Looking back now, I think my mother may have had a premonition that one day, someone might come to visit looking for the old her. Thank you very much for coming. I would like to thank you from the bottom of my heart."

I could feel Linda's thoughts emanating out from the text.

Since Our Interview

Vera's husband Emil's home in Vienna.
This was the family-owned jewelry store

On July 1, 2017, I was standing in front of a building on Taborstrasse in the center of Vienna. In the 1930s, there was a jewelry store on the first floor of this building called "Kronberg." It was the family home of Emil Kronberg, Vera's husband. In December 2015, on the day I met with Linda, I had stared at a picture she showed me. Then she said, "This is a picture of the store in Vienna. You can see the 'Kronberg' sign. It was attacked and destroyed in the Kristallnacht (Crystal Night) incident that occurred on November 9, 1938. Fortunately, my father had been out of the country before this incident, so he was not physically harmed. As a Jew, I think my father's life was also a great hardship."

Of course, there was no sign of "Kronberg" now, and the whole building must have been rebuilt. The adjacent building, however, was different in appearance, but clearly still intact. I heard that many of the stores on this street were owned by Jews. Kristallnacht must have been an appalling incident too dreadful to watch.

As I was imagining this, I was reminded of a movie I saw recently.

It was *Woman in Gold*, produced in 2015. The film is based on the true story of the recapture of "Portrait of Adele Bloch-Bauer I," a masterpiece by Austrian painter Gustav Klimt. The protagonist was Maria Altman, an elderly Jewish woman who successfully sued the Austrian government to regain family possessions that were stolen by the Nazis, including the famous painting of her aunt. Maria Altman was born into a wealthy Jewish family in Vienna. She had been forced to flee to America to be safe from the looming Nazi persecution.

The story of Vera and her husband, Emil Kronberg, overlapped in my mind with events from the film.

When I interviewed Linda, she had shown me her parents' passports. It was thanks to the passports that she was able to tell me more about Vera's activities.

Let's take a look at the passport of Linda's father, Mr. Kronberg.

It was issued on September 5, 1940. Since Austria had been annexed by Germany at that time, the cover of the passport was decorated with the words "DEUTSCHES REICH" (German State) and the emblem of an eagle and *Hakenkreuz* (swastika), which was quite intimidating. Furthermore, when you turned the cover, you would see the abominable vermilion letter "J" on the right-hand page. It is a symbol of humiliation and hardship for the Jewish people.

Linda's story continues.

"My father, who was a jeweler, came to Norway before World War II and did business with my grandfather, who owned a store, and that's when he met my mother. She didn't tell me much about her and my father's relationship at that time, but one day they went to see some event together. My guess is that's when my father started to develop a liking for my mother.

"I never knew how they came to the United States after that. He was married at that time, but his marriage was not going well, and they divorced shortly after they came to the United Staes. Then he married my mother.

"In fact, I used to think that my father and mother came to America separately, but recently I found out through some research that they arrived in San Francisco from Yokohama, Japan on the same ship. It sounds like something that would appear in a novel."

Emil's passport (top and bottom)

From his passport, I would like to trace the footsteps of Vera's husband, who played the role of guardian angel for her after her perilous experiences.

January 27, 1941:	Obtains a visa to the United States at the US Embassy in Stockholm (four days before Vera)
January 29, 1941:	Obtains a transit visa through Japan at the Japanese Embassy in Stockholm. On the same day, obtains a visa to enter the USSR at the USSR Delegation (six days before Vera)
February 5, 1941:	Purchases 750 US dollars at the Scandinavian Bank in Stockholm*
February 23, 1941:	Enters Japan at Tsuruga, Fukui Prefecture (accompanied by Vera)
March 6, 1941:	Departs Yokohama aboard the Nippon Yusen *Tatsuta Maru* (accompanied by Vera)
March 20, 1941:	Arrives in San Francisco (accompanied by Vera)

Here, I would like to point out that I am not inquiring out of curiosity, but out of a desire to record the history of a man and a woman who were tossed about by fate.

About to be victims of the Nazi regime, they had a fateful encounter, were forced to leave their homelands, landed in Tsuruga on a Japanese ship as refugees while huddling together, and escaped to the United States on another Japanese ship.

In this sense, we can say that the Japanese nation played a major role in sending them safely to the land of the free.

Addendum

In closing this chapter, I would like to add the following.

I described how five people were identified. Except for Zosia in part 1, all the others in parts 2 to 5 were identified with a great deal of help from two of my acquaintances, Mr. Kiyotaka Fukushima of Kamakura, Japan, and Mr. Mark Halpern of Pennsylvania. They met at the convention of the International Association of Jewish Genealogical Societies held in Boston in

---

* The exchange rate between the US dollar and the Japanese yen at that time was 4.267 yen to the dollar (Bank of Japan Centennial History), and 750 dollars was 3200 yen. Since the starting salary for a civil servant with a college degree at the time was about 75 yen, 750 dollars would be about 8.5 million yen today.

2013. Later, in January 2016, Mr. Fukushima and I became acquainted, and a system of triangular cooperation was formed.

I would like once again to express my gratitude to them.

With Mark

With Taka-san

4

Jan Zwartendijk, Consul of the Netherlands in Kaunas

The term "visas for life" has now become synonymous with Chiune Sugihara, and as this trend intensifies, more and more people sing his praises. There are movies, TV dramas, documentaries, variety shows, school textbooks, musicals, and even operas and one-man shows.

Of course, it is fine to praise the greatness of our fellow countrymen, but in doing so, as I mentioned in the Introduction, we should not forget that there were other people besides Chiune Sugihara who saved Jews at that time.

Jan Zwartendijk

I remember that I came to know about Jan Zwartendijk before 2010, when I started to prepare for writing my previous book, *Visas of Life and the Epic Journey.*

In the process of researching various materials, I learned that Sugihara Chiune was able to issue Japanese transit visas to Jews because of the existence of the "Curaçao visas" issued by the Dutch consul, Zwartendijk. At the time, I was only aware of it to the extent that I thought, "I see, that's how it happened," and I could not discuss it in detail in my previous book.

After that, I tried to learn more about him little by little, and eventually I had a chance to understand in depth what he did.

This occurred when I read a memoir left by Zwartendijk's eldest son. The following passage in particular left a deep impression on me.

"From 1940 to 1941, thousands of Jewish refugees fled Europe from Poland through Lithuania. It is well known that Mr. Sugihara played a major role in this. But that was only part of that escape drama."

This sentence strangely stuck in my mind as I wondered what he meant by "only a part of the escape drama." As I learned more about the circumstances, I felt that we could not talk about the Sugihara visas without talking about the Curaçao visas.

In July of 1940, a large number of Jewish refugees came to the consulate of Chiune Sugihara. In order for him to issue visas for these Jews to pass through Japan, they had to have permission to enter the country where they were going to after arriving in Japan. At that time, the Dutch-controlled island of Curaçao in the Caribbean could be reached without a visa, and this played a role in opening the door to a breakthrough. These were the so-called Curaçao visas, and it was Zwartendijk who issued them.

I'm certain that those who are familiar with the Sugihara visas already know something about this story, but not much is known about the details. I was one of the lucky ones to hear the story directly from a person who was saved by a Curaçao visa.

This is the story.

Peppy Sternheim was a Jewish woman born in 1911. Originally a Dutch citizen, Peppy became a Polish citizen after marrying Polish author Isaac Lewin. When World War II broke out, Peppy and her family escaped from Lodz, Poland's second largest city at the time, to Lithuania. Peppy's mother and brother, who were visiting from Holland, fled with them.

Peppy (right) and Nathan (left), mother and son

However, Peppy had the foresight to realize that Lithuania was no longer safe. She asked Zwartendijk to give her a visa to enter Java in the Dutch East Indies (now Indonesia).

At first, Zwartendijk refused to grant Peppy a visa because she had already lost her Dutch citizenship. She then sent a letter of appeal directly to the Dutch ambassador, de Decker, Zwartendijk's superior, who was at that time stationed in Riga, the capital of Latvia.

De Decker politely refused, saying that the visa-issuing service had been suspended. But Peppy did not give up and desperately persisted. She argued that she had been a Dutch citizen in the past, and that her mother and brother, who had fled Poland with her, were Dutch citizens.

De Decker, who understood the situation, explained that they could enter either the Dutch Caribbean island of Curaçao or Suriname in South America without visas, but that the local Dutch governor would make the final decision on whether to grant their entry.

In that case, Peppy thought, even though her mother and brother, who were Dutch citizens, would be allowed to enter, there was a strong possibility that the Lewin family, who were Polish citizens, would not. It was then that her uncommon resourcefulness came into play.

She asked de Decker, "Please don't write the second part about the entry permit and just write the first sentence, *No visa is required to travel to Dutch Curaçao and Suriname.*"

Ambassador de Decker

De Decker accepted Peppy's plea and wrote what she asked in her husband's passport on July 11, 1940. (See photo below.) Then, with the handwritten certificate of the Dutch ambassador, she again requested a meeting with Zwartendijk.

Zwartendijk copied exactly what his boss, de Decker, had written on her husband Isaac Lewin's passage permit. (The passage permit was the paper issued to refugees by the Lithuanian government to replace a passport. See photo below.) It was July 22, 1940.

Four days later, on July 26, Mr. and Mrs. Lewin visited the Japanese Consulate with a passage permit to enter Curaçao and received a transit visa to Japan from Chiune Sugihara. (The sequence of the visa issuance is shown in the photo.)

The sequence of visa issuances in 1940: July 11: Ambassador de Decker (left); July 22: Consul Zwartendijk (center); July 26: Deputy Consul Sugihara (right)

By the way, I had the opportunity to attend the opening ceremony of the "Courage to Remember—Holocaust Exhibition: The Bravery of Anne Frank and Chiune Sugihara," held at the Tokyo Metropolitan Theater in Ikebukuro in October 2015. The Dutch and Lithuanian ambassadors were among the guests of honor at the event, and in their speeches, both ambassadors referred to Zwartendijk, saying, "Just like Mr. Sugihara, there was a Dutch diplomat who issued visas for Jews."

A few days later, I visited the Dutch Embassy. I told them that I wanted to know more about Zwartendijk, and the public relations officer warmly welcomed me. He made every effort to fulfill my wish to meet the family. Unfortunately, Zwartendijk's eldest son, who wrote the memoir, passed away in 2014, but through the Dutch Ministry of Foreign Affairs in the Netherlands, I was able to be introduced to his second son, Robert.

I immediately started exchanging emails with him.

He said, "I am very glad that you think that way about our father. While there is a worldwide movement to honor Mr. Sugihara, my father has not been mentioned at all. That disturbs us as a family."

One year and eight months later, in June 2017, I finally had a chance to meet with Robert. It took about an hour from Amsterdam by train and bus. Robert's house was located in a tranquil residential area in a quiet town.

With Robert (June 2017)

"My father helped Jewish refugees out of his human benevolence, and I'm sure he didn't want his achievements to be overemphasized. But it is a pity that his deeds have not received any attention at all."

In these words, I could feel the complicated emotions of the bereaved family.

Why, then, were Zwartendijk's achievements not known even in his home country? One of the reasons is that, as mentioned earlier, the Curaçao visas were not legitimate ones, but were created as a matter of convenience.

For this reason, in later years, the Dutch government took the position that "the government did not approve of the issuance of the Curaçao visas." In other words, the government could not justify the action of Zwartendijk and could not openly recognize it.

Another reason that Zwartendijk's actions were not publicized in the Netherlands was the world situation at the time.

In May 1940, the Netherlands was occupied by Nazi Germany. What would have happened if the Germans had found out that the Dutch consuls had helped Jewish refugees to escape? They might have been shot for treason at any time. The Curaçao visas were indeed "visas for life" issued by the Dutch consul at the risk of his own life.

In August of that year, the Dutch Consulate in Kaunas was closed, and Zwartendijk returned home with his family. From that time until the end of the war in 1945, the family must have lived in seclusion.

Even after the war, the fact that Zwartendijk had issued visas to Jewish refugees was kept secret for a long time, and even after the act finally became known to the public, the Dutch government did not acknowledge it.

Zwartendijk passed away in 1976 and it was not until 1997, 21 years after his death, that the Israeli government belatedly recognized his achievements and awarded him Yad Vashem's title of "Righteous Among the Nations."

On the other hand, Chiune Sugihara was awarded the title in 1985, the year before his death, so it can be said that he was very fortunate in the sense that his achievements were recognized during his lifetime.

Fortunately, there was a very happy event for the Zwartendijk family. On June 15, 2018, twenty-one years after Jan Zwartendijk received the award from Yad Vashem, a grand ceremony was held in Kaunas to honor Zwartendijk. The king of the Netherlands and the president of Lithuania attended the event. Of course, Robert and his sister Edith were invited to the ceremony. I wonder how they must have felt as bereaved family members.

Robert delivering a speech of gratitude at the ceremony
honoring Jan Zwartendijk (June 15, 2018)

Later, Robert sent me his impressions of the ceremony, which I would like to introduce below.

Hello Akira!

Actually, the Ceremony was on the 15th of June.

It was great that, apart from my 91-year-old sister Edith who lives in France, my eldest son Bas with his wife Ilone (living in the Netherlands) and my youngest son David with his wife Jennifer and son Noah (living in the USA), all came over to Lithuania for the event.

We were very grateful to Ambassador van der Lingen for his tireless efforts in realizing this fine Monument in honor of my father and remembering the 2,200 lives saved.

We all felt very honored that King Willem Alexander of the Netherlands, President Grybauskaitė of Lithuania, the Mayor of Kaunas and a number of dignitaries assisted in the Ceremony.

It is a truly impressive monument consisting of a circle of 2,200 small sticks of LED lights which are lit 24/24.

The circle is fixed about 3 meters in the air right in front of my father's office.

Below the circle in the pavement there is a plaque with my father's name, and it is also lit 24/24.

I like the fact that it is not so much about the glorification of my father but rather the symbolic meaning that in taking the right decision so many lives were saved.

Personal regards,

Rob

I should mention that about forty copies of the visas are kept at the Sugihara Chiune Memorial Museum in Yaotsu Town, Gifu Prefecture, Chiune Sugihara's hometown. Sugihara visas and the Curaçao visas are shown side by side and it is very interesting to see the process by reading the dates of each visa. It is well known that both Zwartendijk and Sugihara started out with handwritten visas, but due to the flood of applications, they started using stamps. I found out from looking at these visas that Zwartendijk switched to stamps on July 24 and Sugihara on August 2. Both of them issued over 2,000 visas in a short period of time, and one can only imagine how much work it must have been.

It is also a curious coincidence that the consuls of the two countries issued a large number of visas for Jewish refugees from a humanitarian perspective at the exact same time. Moreover, various documents indicate that the two men never met in person. How is it possible that such a thing could have been done without any meeting? I found it hard to believe.

In June 2016, I attended an event in Los Angeles related to Chiune Sugihara, with Nathan Lewin, a lawyer who is the son of Peppy Sternheim Lewin. For me, it was a unique opportunity to solve the question.

With Nathan Lewin (July 2016)

"My mother told me that they must have met at some point and had some sort of meeting, but I was not there myself, so I don't know the truth," was Mr. Lewin's reply.

Rather than answering that question, he enthusiastically told me how the Curaçao visa came to be. It was him whom I mentioned previously as the "person who was saved by the visa."

The following is an exchange between Mr. Lewin and me.

Kitade: "Everyone who survived on the Sugihara visa says, 'If it were not for Mr. Sugihara, my family and I would not be alive today.' But from listening to your story, I don't think we should forget about Mr. Zwartendijk's existence."

Mr. Lewin: "That's right. And I must also add the understanding and wisdom of Ambassador de Decker."

Kitade: "Or more precisely, if it weren't for the tenacity of your mother ..."

Mr. Lewin: "Yes, tenacity, or rather determination."

At this point, Mr. Lewin smiled, and his expression was one of satisfaction.

On the other hand, when I asked the same question during my visit to Robert Zwartendijk as mentioned above, he immediately assured me that there was no proof that his father and Chiune Sugihara had met on this matter. He did, however, tell me of an episode that showed there might have been some contact between the two diplomats. It was ...

"Because Zwartendijk switched from handwriting to stamps a week earlier than Sugihara, Jewish refugees with Curaçao visas flooded the Japanese Consulate and formed a long line. Sugihara became frustrated and called the Dutch Consulate. He asked Zwartendijk to slow down the pace of visas because he could not handle them if they were issued too quickly."

Robert also said that his sister told him she often saw Mrs. Sugihara go out in her kimono, as they lived relatively close to each other.

The fact that two diplomats from different countries and different positions unexpectedly worked together to save the lives of Jews could be called a "mystery of history."

The following is a brief history of Jan Zwartendijk in the context of the world situation at the time.

1896:	Born in Rotterdam, the Netherlands
1938:	Assigned to Kaunas as a representative of Philips
May 1940:	Germany invaded the Netherlands
June 1940:	Appointed as consul of the Netherlands in Kaunas
August 1940:	Lithuania annexed by the Soviet Union
September 1940:	Returned to the Netherlands
May 1945:	Germany surrendered
August 1945:	World War II ended
1976:	Died at the age of eighty
1997:	Awarded the Righteous Among the Nations title by Yad Vashem
June 2018:	A ceremony honoring him was held in Kaunas

(Author's note: Zwartendijk's title is sometime rendered as "honorary consul" or "deputy consul," but I used "consul" here for convenience.)

In concluding this chapter, I would like to emphasize that the Jewish exodus that took place in Lithuania over a period of several months from July 1940 was made possible only by the combination of the Sugihara visas and the Curaçao visas. (However, as I discuss in the next chapter, the role of the Soviet authorities at the time probably must also be taken into account.)

Of the many books I have read on the visas for life, one of the most reliable is *Diplomat Heroes of the Holocaust* by Mordecai Paldiel, published by KTAV

Publishing House, Inc., 2007. (I have read its Japanese version, *Holocaust and Diplomat*, published by Jinbunshoin, in 2015.) In the book, the author considers the visa issuance of Zwartendijk and Chiune Sugihara as inseparable.

At the National Holocaust Museum in Vilnius, which I visited three years ago, the photographs of the two men are displayed together as shown in the photo, and their respective achievements are introduced equally.

Display at the National Holocaust Museum in Vilnius (top); display at Sugihara House in Kaunas (bottom)

Also, at the Sugihara House in Kaunas, the room that used to be the office of Chiune Sugihara has been recreated to give visitors a sense of realism.

What was very impressive to me was that the entire wall in one of the rooms was covered to show the achievements of Zwartendijk. (See photos on the previous page.)

Chiune Sugihara Square in Zuiryo High School. Photograph provided by Aichi Board of Education

When I think about the situation in Japan regarding this matter, the first thing that comes to mind is the Sempo Sugihara Memorial at Zuiryo High School in Nagoya, the alma mater of Chiune (Sempo) Sugihara, which I mentioned previously. This monument is excellent from an international perspective in that it does not focus on Chiune Sugihara alone, but also on many other people, including Zwartendijk. I would encourage all readers to visit the site.

Up to this point, you may have noticed that I am very emphatic about Zwartendijk. Actually, there is a reason for this.

A couple of years ago, an English translation of my article on the background of the birth of the Curaçao visa was posted on the English website Japan Forward. A reader wrote in response, making the following statements.

- Zwartendijk was acting according to the orders from his superior de Decker; he did not disobey orders, unlike Sugihara.
- Mr. Chiune Sugihara mentioned in an interview that he never met Mr. Zwartendijk.
- No matter how the refugees came to Mr. Sugihara, he risked his life and disobeyed orders to have visas issued to people without valid documents. There is no need to give credit to anyone else but Mr. Sugihara.
- The reader wondered about the credibility of the author of the article, a journalist who seemed to be just a travel agent.

One of the panels on display. Photograph provided by Aichi Board of Education

- The reader saw this article as unreliable and a disgrace for such a well-established newspaper as the *Japan Forward*.

In Japan, slandering others anonymously on SNS is a big problem and I have been subjected to it.

Apart from my own experience, I am concerned that the words and actions of these blindly believing Sugihara fans are damaging his reputation.

It should be noted, however, that there were some people who received Japanese transit visas without Curaçao visas. Mr. Benjamin Fishoff in chapter 2 is one of those who did not have a Curaçao visa. His number on the Sugihara list is 2070, and his visa was issued on August 21. We can assume that the people right before and after him probably did not have Curaçao visas.

There was also the case of Abram Shmoys, a person I met who had a visa signed on August 29, 1940 by "Chiune Sugihara" even though his name was not on the Sugihara list. Considering these facts, it is undeniable that Sugihara's actions in the latter half of August were clearly based on a humanitarian spirit.

In this respect, Chiune Sugihara was undoubtedly a rare human being.

5

Saburo Nei, Acting Consul General in Vladivostok

The next stop for the Jewish refugees in Europe who had obtained the "Curaçao visa," a prerequisite for going to Japan, and who had been successfully issued a transit visa through Japan by Chiune Sugihara, was Vladivostok, Siberia.

Here, I had a question that I had been wondering about for a long time: *Why did the Soviet authorities allow them to pass through its vast territory to get from Lithuania to Vladivostok? Chiune Sugihara is said to have obtained the approval of the authorities in advance, but were the negotiations that easy? Wasn't Lithuania already occupied by the Soviet Union, and weren't Jewish refugees under their strict control by then?*

Fortunately, my question was answered through the work done by a Russian researcher whom I had met a few years ago, and by what I heard from my acquaintances.

The Soviet Union, which annexed Lithuania in June 1940, wanted to deal with the problem of Jewish refugees fleeing Poland as soon as possible. There were two main reasons for this.

The first one was the economic factor.

According to documents that the researcher obtained from the Russian archives, Intourist, the state-run travel agency, oversaw the movement of Jewish refugees within the Soviet Union, and the income from the Trans-Siberian Railway fares and hotel fees was not insignificant. Vladimir Dekanozov, the former head of the People's Commissariat for Internal Affairs (NKVD, the predecessor of the KGB), was in charge of the management of Jewish refugees at that time. In a letter to his boss, future foreign minister Molotov, Dekanozov reported that he expected to earn 1.5 million dollars. The Soviet Union at the time was certainly grateful for this means of obtaining foreign currency.

The second reason given was that Dekanozov, who had been in charge of foreign intelligence activities during his time in the NKVD, was attempting to turn Jewish refugees into spies and send them around the world. There is a story that a consulate official solicited a Polish Jewish man who came to apply for an exit visa. Placing a pistol on his desk, the official asked if the man were willing to become a spy for the Soviet Union.

At that time, many countries in the world were reluctant to accept Jewish refugees, and the Soviet Union was no exception. Rather, it would have welcomed their departure from Europe. For these reasons, the Soviet authorities were quite generous and quickly allowed them to pass through.

Saburo Nei. Photograph provided by the Saburo Nei Honoring Association

Now, let's move on to the main subject of this chapter, Saburo Nei, who was the acting consul general of the Japanese Consulate General in Vladivostok. Let me begin with a brief introduction to his career.

March, 1902:	Born in Miyazaki Prefecture (present-day Sadohara-cho, Miyazaki City)
March, 1921:	Graduated from Omura Junior High School under the old education system in Nagasaki Prefecture
April, 1921:	Passed the Ministry of Foreign Affairs Foreign Student Recruitment Examination
June, 1921:	Studied in Harbin as a foreign student from the Ministry of Foreign Affairs
April, 1925:	Worked at the Japanese Consulate General in Harbin
November, 1925:	Served at the Japanese Consulate General in Vladivostok. (After this, he worked in Vladivostok twice)
August, 1940:	Served at the Japanese Consulate General in Vladivostok for the fourth time
December 1940:	Became acting consul general
February 1941:	From February 8 to June 2, 1941, corresponded with the Ministry of Foreign Affairs regarding Jewish refugees in Vladivostok

August 1945: The war ended while he was in Japan.

March 1962: Ended his career as a civil servant after serving at the office of the Nagoya Immigration Office

March 1992: Passed away (age ninety)

I first learned about Saburo Nei in 2010, when I began writing my previous book, *Visas of Life and the Epic Journey*. He was introduced in the book *Escape to Freedom: Sugihara Visas and the Jews* (published by Chunichi Shimbun), which I was reading for reference.

The story was about a Jewish student who obtained a Sugihara visa in Kaunas, but of all things, he lost the passport in which it was written.

He went from elation to despair. Still desperate, he made it to Vladivostok and rushed to the Japanese Consulate General. After explaining the situation, Nei, the acting consul general, who oversaw the case, granted him a visa and even sent him to a hotel by sleigh. The student said, "I was thrilled when I received my visa from Sugihara, but I was ecstatic in Vladivostok."

The name "Saburo Nei" entered my mind when I learned about this episode. However, to be honest, I cannot deny that Chiune Sugihara's actions were more important to me at the time.

Then, in the process of searching for materials related to the "Visas for Life," Saburo Nei's name came up frequently. And each time, I came across the expression *omoshirokarazu*. This term means "not agreeable," and can be interpreted as "I respectfully disagree."

Chiune Sugihara issued visas for about a month from the end of July through August of 1940. The number of visas he issued was about 2,000. By the following year, an increasing number of refugees were arriving in Japan with that visa. The Ministry of Foreign Affairs, struggling to cope with the situation, sent frequent telegrams of instruction to the Japanese Embassy in Moscow and the Consulate General of Japan in Vladivostok. The following is an example.

February 19, 1941, from Foreign Minister Yosuke Matsuoka to Acting Consul General Nei:

"We have inquired at the Jewish Association in Kobe, and they have told us that they are unable to take care of the large number of refugees, so you are requested to refrain from issuing visas."

Another letter, dated February 26, also from the foreign minister:

"There are currently about 1,200 refugees in Japan, and we are having difficulty in dealing with them. Therefore, no transit visas to Japan should be issued to refugees in your area."

At the same time, the ambassador to Moscow, Yoshitsugu Tatekawa (introduced in chapter 7), was also instructed to tighten restrictions on the issuance of visas.

Later, on behalf of Matsuoka, who was on a visit to Europe, the Temporary Foreign Minister Fumimaro Konoe issued two extremely strict directives, the first on March 17, 1941 and the second on March 19.

The main points were briefly as follows:

(1) The issuance of transit visas should be limited to Moscow.
(2) All transit visas (including Sugihara visas) issued before December 20 of the previous year shall be re-inspected in Moscow or Vladivostok and shall only be accepted at the ship after being stamped if the entry procedures of the destination country have been completed.
(3) The Soviet authorities shall also be notified of this.
(4) The refugees shall be warned that it will be useless to go to Vladivostok unless they have fulfilled the conditions.

To this, not only Tatekawa but also Nei strongly objected in a telegram dated March 30 (see the photograph below). The aforementioned expression *omoshirokarazu* can be seen in this telegram, which shows the extent of Saburo Nei's determination. Although it is a bit long, I would like to quote the entire text of Nei's telegram. However, I must warn you that I have interpreted some parts because the sentences are based on the terminology and expressions used in the government offices at that time.

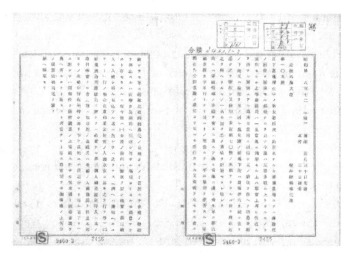

The documents sent from Deputy Consul General Nei to the Temporary Foreign Minister Fumimaro Konoe. Photograph from the Ministry of Foreign Affairs Diplomatic Archives

There are about 100 refugees in Vladivostok at this time, but it appears that the Soviet authorities are planning to restrict their departure.

Therefore, we expect the number of refugees will not be as large as in the future. Once these refugees arrive here, it is virtually impossible for them to return. Because of this, they have been coming to our office every day, appealing their plight, and asking for a transit visa or a stamp. In accordance with your telegram No. 69, we have refused to issue any new visas, and in accordance with your telegram No. 70, we have refused to give any seals of inspection to any of the passengers and have refused to allow them to board the ship.

However, from the standpoint of the prestige of the imperial consulates abroad, I respectfully disagree [omoshirokarazu] with uniformly denying a seal of inspection simply because a third-country visa is for Central America, when a person with an imperial consular visa has come all the way to Vladivostok. Moreover, it is not appropriate to suspend the issuance of visas to those who do not have them just because it simplifies the control of refugees when it is obvious that they cannot return to Moscow. Therefore, in the future, (1) visas should be stamped with extreme caution and only for those who are expected to enter a third country (for example, in the case of those bound for the Dutch territory of Curaçao, upon approval of entry by the Dutch legation in Tokyo). (2) For new applications for transit visas, for those who are certain to have a visa to enter a third country (for example, those who have a Canadian visa or a US entry permit and a boarding ticket from Japan, but are stuck in this country), we may grant transit visas as in the past, after a strict investigation of the conditions. We believe that it would be appropriate to grant transit visas to these people as in the past. Please consider the situation and send us a reply as soon as possible.

The term *omoshirokarazu* is, I feel, an unusually strong word for a Japanese diplomat in a foreign country to use in correspondence with his home ministry. From the sentences before and after, it seems that he understood the situation of the refugees well and wanted to do something about it, which suggests that he had a strong sense of justice and humanitarian spirit.

When I learned the above story about Saburo Nei, I began to think. *When it comes to the Visas for Life, Chiune Sugihara is often in the limelight, but Saburo Nei should also be in the spotlight.*

Since then, whenever I have the opportunity to give a lecture or write, I have tried to mention Saburo Nei as much as possible. However, to be honest, the effort has not gotten much of a response.

Meanwhile, in August 2016, the Saburo Nei Honoring Association was established by local volunteers in Sadohara-cho, Miyazaki City, where Nei was born. In the following year, various facts became known and were picked up by the media.

Gradually, the spotlight began to shine on Saburo Nei.

In September 2019, I visited Sadohara-cho and met with the people of the Association to get a feel for the local atmosphere and explain my perspective.

At the Saburo Nei Honoring Association: From right to left: Hidehiro Fukushima from the association; Yoku Nei, the chairman; Shigeto Tomioka, Saburo Nei's nephew; and the author

"I have been writing articles and giving lectures on Jewish refugees and 'visas for life' as a freelance writer, and through these activities, I have recently come to feel that in Japan, people tend to treat Chiune Sugihara as if he alone saved Jewish refugees. From now on, I would like people to know more about Mr. Saburo Nei."

In response, Mr. Yoku Nei, the chairman of the association, said, "You are absolutely right. We believe that we must spread the word about this splendid man who was born in our hometown."

He expressed his full support. (Incidentally, Chairman Nei is not related to Saburo Nei, although they share the same surname.)

Six months later, on April 6, 2020, something unbelievable happened. It was a single email from Mark Halpern (mentioned in chapter 3), who lives in the United States and whom I have known for several years. Mark specializes in genealogical research of Jewish families and is of great help to me.

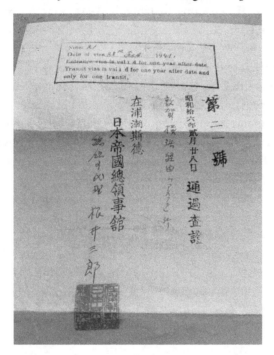

The first time a single visa from Nei was confirmed

"Akira, would you please tell me what the Chinese characters in the attached document mean? The person who asked me is Kim Hydorn, whom you also know."

I took a glance at the attached photo and told myself, *No way!*

As you can see in the photo, which we've included here, it was definitely a transit visa issued on February 28, 1941, with the inscription "Saburo Nei, Acting Consul General, Consulate-General of Japan at Vladivostok." What particularly caught my attention was the beautiful handwriting of "Saburo Nei, Acting Consul General."

I immediately sent a copy of the letter to the office of the Association in Miyazaki to have it looked at.

"We were very surprised to see such a single visa for the first time! If you have any further information, please let us know."

Then came the hard part. I had much to do. First, I informed Mark of the details, and then I contacted an old acquaintance, Kim Hydorn. She had never heard of Saburo Nei until Mark told her about him.

Here, I have to explain a little about Kim.

Kim's mother is named Felicja. Felicja's parents were Simon and Emma Korentajer. These three were Jewish refugees from Poland who fled Europe during World War II and came to Japan in 1941. Like many other refugee families, they stayed in Kobe for a while before being sent to Shanghai, and finally made it to the United States in 1947.

I first came across the names of the three Korentajers on a list of Jewish refugees on file in the Diplomatic Archives of the Ministry of Foreign Affairs (see the top photograph below). The list, compiled in August 1941 by Hyogo Prefecture, documented approximately 300 people who had remained in Kobe at the time. Among them were the three people who were obviously parents and their child. The entry "Felicja, age 4" particularly caught my attention. The name of this little girl stayed with me for a long time.

A few years later, I found the same three names on a list I had obtained from the Dutch Embassy in Tokyo (see the bottom three photographs below). It named seventy-four people who had been sent back to Vladivostok because they were refused landing at Tsuruga Port due to incomplete documents but were finally allowed to enter Japan through the efforts of the then Dutch legation in Tokyo (as described in chapter 2, in the section "Mr. Benjamin Fishoff").

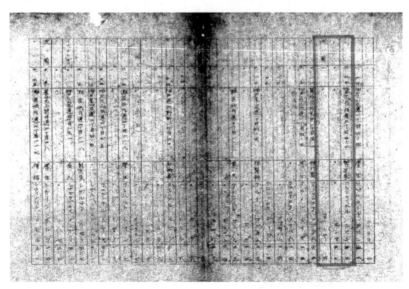

Three people on the Hyogo list

```
The Netherlands Legation hereby certifies that the
undermentioned persons all of Polish nationality do not
need a Netherlands visa in order to proceed to the
Netherlands West-Indies (Curaçao, Surinam, etc.)

1. Beiler Abraham Mojzesz          38. Bursztynarz - Abramczyk Jankiel
2. Goldberg Chaim                  39. Goldberg Szmuilo Morduch
3. Gastner Mirsz                   40. Korentajer Szymon
4. Tunienter Szaja                 41.    "       Emma
5. Seroka Szymon                   42.    "       Felicja
6. Ruchlejmer Izak                 43. Fuks Abram
7. Szwarcman Szlama Uszer          44.  "  Szajna Hendla
```

Curaçao immigration certificates nos. 40, 41, 42

Again, the mention of Felicja Korentajer stuck in my mind. *How could a little girl, only four years old, have gone through such a difficult journey to come to Japan? With the help of the letters of her name, perhaps I can find out where she is now.*

The day finally came in June 2018. When I was searching the Internet for "Korentajer," I unexpectedly got a hit on Emma Korentajer. It was an article in a local newspaper from the town of Oxnard, California, which mentioned a woman named Phyllis Dimant. It rang a bell, and I immediately contacted Mark.

"Mark," I said, "I think that Felicja may have married and become Phyllis Dimant. Can you look into it?"

His reply came in no time.

"Akira, you were right. To my surprise, her daughter was Kim, whom I had met on a recent trip to Poland with my wife. It's such a strange thing, isn't it? I hope you will get in touch with Kim."

This is how I got to know her. She sent me some photos of her mother, Felicja, from her time in Shanghai, but we didn't communicate any further after that.

And then, two years later, through a piece of paper, we reconnected. It was as if we were being guided by some invisible thread. Kim told me that she had visited the Sugihara House in Kaunas last year. (The Japanese Consulate from that time is now a memorial hall.) Kim had checked the Sugihara list carefully but could not find the names of her family. She was surprised at the emergence of another diplomat, Saburo Nei, but at the same time pleased to know the truth. Thus, after a gap of two years, she and I began to frequently exchange emails.

From the information and documents Kim provided me, I learned the following facts about her family.

Grandfather: Simon Korentajer (born in Warsaw on August 31, 1908)
Grandmother: Emma (born in Kaunas on May 27, 1904)
Mother: Felicja (born in Warsaw on March 24, 1937)
The route of their escape journey:

On September 1, 1939, they escaped to Lithuania when the Nazis invaded Poland.

In December, they registered as refugees in Kaunas.

On February 2, 1941, Mr. Korentajer applied for an immigrant visa at the US Embassy in Moscow, which was denied on February 6.

They then went to Vladivostok by Trans-Siberian Railway. On February 28, they received transit visas to Japan from Acting Counsel General Saburo Nei. They arrived in Tsuruga on March 29, stayed in Kobe for a while, then moved to Shanghai, where they stayed for six and a half years.

It is noteworthy that the visa number is 21 and the date is written as February 28, 1941. This means that there were 20 visas issued before that date, but so far, no other similar visas have been confirmed. What is even more interesting is that, as mentioned above, Nei had received a telegram from the Ministry of Foreign Affairs on February 26 ordering him to stop issuing visas. Since he could not possibly have overlooked this communication, did he dare to ignore his instructions?

On a related note, apart from visas, there is a document called a travel certificate. It has the same effect as a visa, and you can think of it as a document that allows you to travel abroad. I have a copy of this document, and I can see Saburo Nei's name on it as well. The date is March 16, 1941, and it is number 9. The entries are, in order, first and last name (illegible), year of birth (1922), occupation (student), nationality (Poland), destination (United States of America), landing place in Japan (Tsuruga), and port of embarkation (Vladivostok). (Author's note: Unfortunately, due to copyright issues, I am unable to post a photograph of this copy.)

What can be inferred from the above is that, after the issuance of visa no. 21, Nei stopped issuing visas and switched to travel certificates in accordance with an instruction from the Ministry. He started issuing them with number 1. This was probably after March 1. It is not at all unreasonable to think that nine certificates were issued in a period of about two weeks. In fact, it is quite convincing. So how many more travel certificates were issued? We don't know that at the moment. As with the visas, the other documents have not been confirmed.

Another task that Nei was involved in was the "seal inspection" that the Ministry of Foreign Affairs instructed him to perform for the Jewish refugees going to Japan. The photo below is a document preserved in the Israel National Archives and Records Administration. Top left is the Sugihara visa, which was issued on August 21, 1940. In the center on the right side is Nei's seal of approval. The date is April 19, 1941, which is probably near the end of the Jewish refugees' escape from Europe.

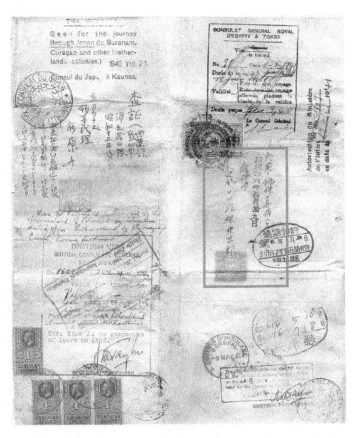

Saburo Nei's stamps. Photographs provided by Israel State Archives

How many visas did Nei issue, how many travel certificates did he write, and how many did he stamp? Judging from the confirmed documents, there seems to be a big difference from the performance of Chiune Sugihara, who issued more than 2,000 visas.

However, a large number does not always indicate its significance. Professor Yakov Zinberg of Kokushikan University, who is a researcher of Saburo Nei, says, "Mr. Nei, who had experienced working in Vladivostok four times, can be considered as more knowledgeable about the Soviet Union than Sugihara. Around April 13, 1941, when the Soviet-Japanese Neutrality Treaty was signed, it was necessary for Japan to suppress information from the Soviet side, and it is quite possible that Nei was involved in this. At the very least, he was the most 'experienced' of those involved at the time."

As for the revelation of the existence of the hitherto unknown Nei visas, I played the role of the discoverer due to the aforementioned circumstances.

This is a very fortunate thing for me, as I have always been aware that there were people other than Chiune Sugihara who extended a helping hand to Jewish refugees, and I have been advocating that they should also be highlighted. I hope that this will be an opportunity for further research on Saburo Nei by his Honoring Association.

To conclude this chapter, I would like to introduce some old and recent photos of the Korentejer family, who were helped by the Nei visas.

Korentajer family around 1950. From left to right: Simon, Felicja, and Emma

Kobe, 1941. From left to right: Paster Shiro Seto, Felicja, Emma, Mrs. Seto, three people on their right unknown. Second row: Simon on the right, left unknown

At Felicja's grandchild's wedding (2015). Felicja is in the center. To her left is Kim, to her right is her eldest daughter, Deborah

6

N. A. J. de Voogd, Consul of the Netherlands in Kobe, Later Ambassador of the Netherlands to Japan

Do you recall the *Amakusa Maru* Incident?

I would like to remind you of the story told by Mr. Benjamin Fishoff, whom I introduced in chapter 2. Yes, it is the story of a group of seventy-four people who were denied entry into Japan at Tsuruga because of incomplete documents, were sent back to Vladivostok, returned to Tsuruga, and were finally allowed to land.

During his interview, Mr. Fishoff surprised me by stating three dates from memory, without looking at anything: March 13, 16, and 23, 1941. He talked about what happened seventy years ago as if it were yesterday!

Now, here are excerpts from related articles in the *Fukui Shimbun* published during the *Amakusa Maru* incident.

> **Tuesday, March 18, 1941, evening edition, page 2**
> **Scenes of Tears on Board / Jews Repatriated by** *Amakusa Maru*
> The European-Asian liaison ship *Amakusa Maru* departed Tsuruga at 2 p.m. on the 16th, carrying seventy-nine passengers from Japan and abroad, and sailed directly to Vladivostok. ...
> On the same ship there were seventy-four Jews, who had been wandering to avoid the ravages of war in Europe and were repatriated to Vladivostok on the 13th for lack of visas and money. When these refugees found out about the repatriation, some of

them began to cry, and scenes of tragedy were shown repeatedly throughout the ship.

Tuesday, March 25, 1941, evening edition, page 2
Jews Repatriated Again / *Amakusa Maru* Lands in Tsuruga
The European-Asian liaison ship *Amakusa Maru* arrived at Tsuruga at 9 a.m. on March 23. . . . One hundred and ninety-seven Jews, who had escaped the ravages of war in Europe and were continuing their wandering journey, came on the same ship; among them were the seventy-four Jews who had been sent back to Vladivostok on the 16th. The entire group was allowed to land on the afternoon of the same day.

So, how was this group allowed to land?
Let's start with the origin of the incident.
On March 15, 1941, a letter of request was sent to the director of the Third Section, US Bureau, Japanese Ministry of Foreign Affairs. The sender, Anatole Ponevejsky, president of the Kobe Jewish Association, made the following appeal.

"Of the Jews who were on the *Amakusa Maru*, which arrived in Tsuruga on the 13th, about ninety have already obtained transit visas from the Japanese consul [Author's note: Sugihara visas], but because they do not have visas from their destination countries, they have been banned from landing and will be repatriated [Author's note: to Vladivostok] tomorrow, on the 16th. However, some of them have already been approved for entry by the authorities of their destination countries, and we will take responsibility for their removal from Japan within a short period of time. Therefore, please negotiate with the personnel in charge of the Ministry of the Interior and consider giving permission upon their landing."

In the meantime, the acting consul general of Vladivostok, Mr. Nei, reported the following on March 19.

The captain of the *Amakusa Maru* discovered that the number of passengers exceeded the capacity of the ship after the sailing procedures were completed, and requested that the excess passengers disembark, as it was impossible to sail with them. The Soviet officials claimed that according to Soviet regulations, they could not allow passengers to disembark for any reason after the sailing procedures were completed, and they tried to leave the ship. If the Soviet officials pull out, the ship will have no choice but to postpone the sailing due to the loss of communication between the Soviet authorities and our office, which will result in a shortage of food for the many passengers and crew. So, the captain decided to sail, and dispatched our office to ask for issuance of permission for a temporary excess of passengers. We sent our staff to the ship to investigate the situation and negotiated with the Soviet officials to disembark the excess passengers, but they stubbornly refused to comply with our request under the shield of Soviet regulations. Therefore, responding to the captain's plea, we issued this certificate as a temporary measure.

A telegram from Ambassador Tatekawa in Moscow to Foreign Minister Konoe dated March 20 also arrived.

"On March 19, the acting director of the consular department of the Soviet Union sent a request to our office staff. According to it, seventy-four refugees from the *Amakusa Maru* have returned to Vladivostok and are currently on board the ship after being refused permission to land in Tsuruga due to the lack of American visas, but because these refugees have Japanese visas, they asked us to take the necessary measures to allow them to land in Japan. I would like you to send me a reply as to how I should respond."

In response, Foreign Minister Konoe sent a reply to Ambassador Tatekawa dated March 25.

"On March 23, seventy-four refugees arrived in Tsuruga again on the *Amakusa Maru*, and the Dutch legation in Tokyo, in response to the pleas of the Jewish community, assured that they would be allowed to enter Curaçao in the Dutch West Indies. Therefore, we granted them permission to land."

There is no discrepancy at all between the contents of the aforementioned three exchanges and the articles in the *Fukui Shimbun*. It can be seen that this was a major event in the drama of the transport of Jewish refugees between Vladivostok and Tsuruga.

Anyway, what a wonderful memory Mr. Fishoff has!

This is the background of the *Amakusa Maru* incident. Now, I would like to move on to the second part, the core of the story.

In fact, the seventy-four refugees were able to land safely in Japan due to the efforts of one diplomat. His name is N. A. J. de Voogd. In 1940, de Voogd was the consul of the Dutch Consulate in Kobe. The telegram quoted above from Foreign Minister Konoe to Ambassador Tatekawa mentioned the guarantee by the Dutch legation in Tokyo; de Voogd was the one who was deeply involved in this matter.

N. A. J. de Voogd

First, I would like to briefly give his biography, followed by a detailed description of the events that followed.

1899:	Born in Kats, the Netherlands
1927–1930:	Interpreter at the Dutch legation in Tokyo
1931–1934:	Lectured at universities in Kyoto and Osaka while studying the Japanese language.
1934–1935:	Second-class interpreter at the Dutch Consulate in Kobe. (During this period, in the radio room he set up in his residence, he monitored the transmissions of Dutch and British ships as he tried to grasp the situation in Europe at that time.)
1940–1941:	Consul of the Dutch Consulate in Kobe
1960–1965:	Ambassador to Japan (stationed in Tokyo)
1977:	Passed away at the age of seventy-eight

N. A. J. de Voogd was a man who had a surprisingly long history with Japan.

De Voogd is still remembered in the Dutch Ministry of Foreign Affairs as a diplomat with extensive knowledge of the languages, cultures, religions, and customs of the countries where he served.

At the age of sixteen, he became passionate about radio and also about following his father's wish that he become a doctor. He went on to study medicine, but illness interrupted his studies and gave him the opportunity to become a radio communications operator, which he had always wanted to do. In the meantime, he learned Japanese and Chinese, and entered the Department of Interpretation attached to the Ministry of Foreign Affairs to train diplomats. Yet, he always strived to master communications technology.

When de Voogd began his service in Japan, the legation in Tokyo (which at that time had not yet been upgraded to an embassy) was still headed by Major General Pabst, who had been appointed in 1923. The Consulate General in Kobe, in the meantime, was headed by Consul General Pennink. He was not loyal to his position in general, and decided everything by himself, thus bypassing Pabst in Tokyo.

At the time, Kobe was exporting Japanese bicycles, sewing machines, and cameras for trade with Batavia and Surabaya, and Consul General Pennink devoted himself to that business, leaving consular duties to de Voogd.

When the seventy-four Jewish refugees were forcefully returned to Vladivostok because they did not have visas for a third country, a young Dutchman named Nathan Gutwirth came to Dutch Consul de Voogd for help. I'd like to briefly tell you about him.

Gutwirth was born in Antwerp, Belgium in 1916 to Orthodox Jewish parents, and later moved to Scheveningen, the Netherlands, where he became a Dutch citizen. Later, he studied Talmud in the Telz Yeshiva in Lithuania where he met Jan Zwartendijk, about whom I wrote in chapter 4. As they were both Dutch, they became close friends. When Lithuania was annexed by the Soviet Union in June 1940, he decided to flee Europe and received a visa for Curaçao from Zwartendijk. Next, he obtained a transit visa to Japan from Chiune Sugihara, which enabled him to reach Japan safely.

A short time after arriving in Japan, Gutwirth received news of the seventy-four Jewish refugees and tried to help these fellow Jews who were in trouble. Although he anticipated no difficulty for himself in leaving Japan with his "Dutch visa," he negotiated ardently with de Voogd on behalf of these seventy-four refugees.

In response to Gutwirth's plea for help, de Voogd replied that he could not do anything without permission from the minister in Tokyo. Gutwirth then showed de Voogd a letter from Ambassador de Decker in Riga about whom I also wrote in chapter 4. De Voogd thought it over for a while and told Gutwirth the letter would do.

Meanwhile, the captain of the *Amakusa Maru*, with the seventy-four refugees on board, had decided not to disembark them in Vladivostok. However, he needed to be informed about what to do with them. He asked the consul to let him know by radio as soon as possible.

Then, de Voogd gave Gutwirth a form with the Dutch Consulate's letterhead and asked him to fill in the necessary information about the seventy-four refugees. With the help of a friend, Gutwirth typed it up and delivered it to de Voogd's house.

The details of what happened during this time are not clear, but my guess is that the following events took place: carrying the completed document, de Voogd went to the legation in Tokyo and requested Pabst's approval and signature. Pabst accused de Voogd of acting far beyond his authority. However, he did not refuse to sign. He had not taken any active part in resolving the tensions that were then developing between the Netherlands and Japan. Deciding that now was the time to make amends, he signed at the bottom of the list of seventy-four names.

As you can see in the photo, the contents are as follows:

> The Netherlands Delegation hereby certifies that the following Polish nationals do not require a Dutch visa to enter the Dutch West Indies (Curaçao, Suriname, etc.).
> List of 74 names
Tokyo, March 18, 1941
J. C. Pabst, Minister of the Netherlands

The list of the seventy-four refugees (Dutch National Library, no. 2,05.65.01:136). Photograph provided by the Dutch Embassy in Japan

With this signed list, de Voogd left for Tsuruga later that day. He contacted the captain of the *Amakusa Maru* by radio from the Tsuruga office of the shipping company (Nihonkai Kisen) and told him what had happened. The next day, the captain informed the Soviet authorities that the visas for the seventy-four people had been issued and they could now enter Japan.

This led to the aforementioned telegram dated March 25 from Foreign Minister Konoe to Ambassador Tatekawa.

In the end, Pabst took no disciplinary action against de Voogd. This may have been because Gutwirth, who worked with de Voogd at the time, publicly stated: "It was not a representative of the War Victims Relief Committee [Author's note: organized by the Polish Embassy], who made radio contact with the *Amakusa Maru* at the shipping company's office in Tsuruga. It was Consul de Voogd, using Morse code, who took on the role of radio operator."

Gutwirth kept in touch with de Voogd until he passed away in 1977, always addressing him as "Mr." and his wife as "Ma'am" to show his respect.

This "Ma'am" was Amarintia de Vries. She and de Voogd were married in 1930. She was as compassionate and purposeful as her husband in helping Jewish refugees in Kobe.

One example of this involved a man named Chaim Nussbaum, who was born in 1909 near Auschwitz. He met Nathan Gutwirth when they were both young. Nussbaum later moved to Lithuania with his wife, children, and his brother in 1939. There, on Gutwirth's recommendation, he obtained a Curaçao visa and a Sugihara visa (Author's note: no. 1630) in August 1940. At the end of November, they boarded the Trans-Siberian Railway and finally arrived in Kobe via Vladivostok and Tsuruga. A few days later, Chaim's wife Rachel gave birth. The newborn baby died later that day. The hardships of their escape were the cause. Not knowing how to inform Kobe City Hall of the death, Chaim called the consulate.

When she received the news, Amarintia immediately sent a trusted doctor to Rachel's side. Thanks to Amarintia's help, Rachel survived. Consul de Voogd also hired an experienced nurse who had worked in Singapore for several years. In addition, he made sure to have fruit brought to her twice a day.

After Rachel's recovery, de Voogd tried to get Dutch passports for Chaim and other Jewish refugees so that they could go to the Dutch East Indies. This was not an easy task, however, because the governor of Batavia (present-day Jakarta) did not want people to enter the country unless they had secured jobs there before leaving Japan.

Fortunately, Chaim was a rabbi, and his younger brother Samuel, after some initial difficulties, secured a position as a math teacher through the efforts of de Voogd.

De Voogd and his wife had two sons. Jan was born in 1933, and Bert in 1934, both in Kobe. Jan remembers that, in 1941, his father took a night train from Kobe on business, which may have been related to a "transit visa." And by doing so, he helped at least 200 Jews, but he acted at that time without consulting his boss, the minister. It is certain that Jan is referring to this very episode of the *Amakusa Maru* Incident in the following correspondence.

In a letter to his brother Bert in January 1975, Jan wrote:

Dear Bert,

Recently you asked me why our father was willing to ignore laws and regulations to help so many people, and why he never told anyone about it.

Our father was a firm believer in determining his own actions. He followed three rules:

1. Think from another person's point of view.
2. Respect the spirit rather than the letter of the law.
3. Be always fair in your dealings with people.

De Voogd family while they were in Kobe. Photograph provided by Jan and Bert de Voogd

From your brother, Jan

By the way, I was fortunate enough one day to obtain a copy of the list that de Voogd had prepared despite possible disciplinary action (see photo). I am secretly proud to say that I was the first Japanese to obtain it in recent years (if not, I should be ashamed of my ego).

Here is the story behind this.

As I mentioned in chapter 4, I visited the Dutch Embassy in December 2015, and told the officer in charge, Mr. Ton van Zeeland, about the seventy-four names. He remembered the story well and handed me a copy on my second visit, saying, "Mr. Kitade, I found them in the archives of the Dutch Ministry of Foreign Affairs."

I looked through the list, suppressing my excitement at this unexpected event. The first thing I looked for was, of course, Mr. Fishoff, who had told me this story.

Sure enough, there was the name "Fiszow Chil" at number 20. There was no "Benjamin," but the name on the Sugihara list was "Chil Benjamin Fiszof," so there was no doubt.

Mr. Fishoff's story was, of course, true!

Controlling my excitement, I went through the list in order starting from the top and came across a name I hadn't expected at all: the tenth one, "Altszuler Antonina." It was the woman from the Osako album whom I described in chapter 3. My excitement grew even greater.

As I continued down the list, I came across a set of three names that I had not expected: numbers 40 to 42 were "Korentajer Szymon," "Emma," and

1. Beiler Abraham Mojzesz		38. Bursztynarz – Abramczyk Jankiel	
2. Goldberg Chaim		39. Goldberg Szmuilo Morduch	
3. Gastner Mirsz		40. Korentajer Szymon	
4. Tanienter Szaja		41. " Emma	
5. Seroka Szymon		42. " Felicja	
6. Ruchlejmer Izak		43. Fuks Abram	
7. Szwaroman Szlama Uszer		44. " Szajna Hendla	
8. Lewin Szepsel		45. Kalisz Szymon	
9. Lew Mejer Dawid		46. " Icchok	
10. Altszuler Antonina		47. Epsztein Abram	
11. Krakowski Wolf Abram		48. Bimbad Szloma	
12. Mendeleon Manus		49. Podchlebnik Efraim	
13. Arabczyk Benjamin		50. Finkelsztajn Benjamin	
14. Guberman Efraim		51. Sztyoer Nachman Boruch	
15. Guberman Sara		52. Jakubowicz Moszek Lajzer	
16. Ulrych Baruch		53. Langer Mozes Izak	
17. Wajngarten Jakub Berek		54. Szejnbaum Lejb	
18. Goldberg Boruch Icko		55. Sznajder Nachman	
19. Wajntraub Josek		56. Susel Sosia Mariam	
20. Fiszow Chil		57 Prokosz Szmul	
21. Bryzman Szymon		58. " Perla	
22. Znamirowski Symcha		59. Kandel Abram Josef	

No 10: Antonina; no. 20: Mr. Fishoff; nos. 40–42: the Korentajer family

"Felicja." These were the three members of the Korentajer family I introduced in chapter 5.

I thanked Mr. van Zeeland for his kindness and left the embassy, and even after returning home, my mind was filled with imagining the hardships these five people must have endured during their escape. In March, it was still winter in the Japan Sea and it must have been a difficult voyage for the aging *Amakusa Maru*. Under such circumstances, the ship was sent back to Vladivostok from Tsuruga, where it had once arrived, and the passengers were confined below deck for a while. Mr. Fishoff must have been right when he said in an interview with the *Chunichi Shimbun* that Tsuruga looked like a paradise to him.

Although the other people on this list must have had their own tumultuous dramas, I am inexplicably moved by the fact this voyage was made possible by the "gratuitous act" of the Dutch consul.

Here, too, were the unknown Visas for Life.

The photograph below is of de Voogd presenting his credentials as Dutch ambassador to the emperor of Japan. One can say that this position was the successful culmination of his career as a diplomat.

At the ceremony of the presentation of credentials on March 16, 1960. Photograph provided by Hans de Vries

7

Yoshitsugu Tatekawa, Ambassador to the Soviet Union

Something happened that made me think that this was indeed a chain reaction.

In chapter 5, I introduced the story of the discovery of the lone Nei's visa, and at that time, an English-language newspaper in Japan ran an article about it. Shortly thereafter, I received an email. The sender introduced himself as Rabbi Aaron Kotler. He asked, "Are you the author of *Visas of Life and the Epic Journey*? I have read the book with great interest. Actually, my mother was also helped by a Japanese diplomat. The diplomat was, however, neither Sugihara nor Nei. His name is Yoshitsugu Tatekawa, who later became the Japanese ambassador to Moscow."

It was an unexpected email, and I was grateful for his offer to send information about his mother if I were interested. I was eager to find out what it was all about, and without hesitation, I replied, "I'm looking forward to hearing from you."

By the way, it was the November 2013 issue of *Rekishi Kaido* (Road of History), which introduced me to Yoshitsugu Tatekawa. It was a Sugihara special issue, entitled "Sugihara Chiune and the Samurai." It included an article with the headline, "Another Samurai Who Fiercely Protested 'We Must Reconsider.'" This was my first encounter with the personage of Yoshitsugu Tatekawa, who had once served as a lieutenant general in the army, becoming a diplomat in his later years. Since then, I have occasionally come across his name in related materials, but all of these encounters have been transient.

Then, on June 9, I suddenly received this email, which at once brought me closer to Yoshitsugu Tatekawa.

Before I talk about Mr. Tatekawa, I would like to chronologically summarize the life of Rabbi Kotler's mother, Rischel, as Rabbi Kotler told it to me.

1923:	Born in Memel, today called Klaipeda, Lithuania, as Rischel Friedman
December 22, 1940:	Engaged to Shneur Kotler. Immediately afterward, he fled alone to Palestine via Odessa and Turkey, where he arrived on January 8, 1941)
December 31, 1940:	Married a German named Josef Moddel, in order to secure an exit visa from the Soviet Union
March 8, 1941:	Obtained a transit visa at the Japanese Embassy in Moscow
March 13, 1941:	Left Moscow for Vladivostok
March 23, 1941:	Landed in Tsuruga
March 23, 1941:	Obtained permission from Hyogo Prefecture to stay in Japan until June 5
August 31, 1941:	Obtained permission to leave Kobe for Shanghai
November 24, 1941:	Obtained permission to stay in Shanghai from the German Consulate in Shanghai
March 23, 1942 (or February 1944):	Divorced Josef Moddel
March 17, 1945:	Married Baruch Leib Sassoon in order to gain permission to enter Canada as his "spouse"
June 6, 1946:	Obtained permission to leave Shanghai
May 21, 1947:	Entered the United States via Canada
November 5, 1947:	Divorced Sassoon
January 19, 1949:	Married Shneur Kotler (eight years after their engagement)
July 19, 2015:	Passed away at age ninety-two

Rischel (right) with her parents and younger sister

This is the history of Rischel's activities that I was able to discern from the copy of her passport sent to me by Rabbi Kotler. I was surprised that she had married twice before arriving in the United States and that she was only seventeen at the time of her first wedding. Her parents, who remained in Lithuania, later became victims of the Holocaust, her father massacred in October 1941 and her mother killed in August 1944. I can sense the desperation of this young woman as she tried to escape from the imminent danger of death.

In such a harsh situation, an event occurred that determined her fate. It was on the night of March 8, 1941.

Rischel stood in front of the Japanese Embassy in Moscow. There were other people in line at the gate. She called out to the guard in English. Surprised that the relatively well-dressed young woman could speak English, the guard opened the gate only for her. When she entered the building, she was greeted by a clerk who seemed to be a secretary. "I need a visa for Japan," she said. After a while, a man wearing what looked like a fine silk kimono came down the stairs. He listened intensely to her plea, pondered for a few moments, then stamped a visa in her passport and signed himself "Yoshitsugu Tatekawa."

"There are still others outside the gate," she said. The person then invited them in as well.

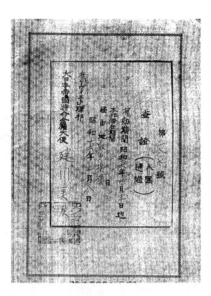

Transit visa signed by Yoshitsugu Tatekawa

It is clear from the stamp of Fukui Prefecture's "transit permit" on her passport that she landed in Tsuruga on March 23, 1941. This means that she was definitely on the *Amakusa Maru* at the time of the *Amakusa Maru* incident described in the previous chapter. The Hyogo Prefecture's "entry permit" stamp on the same page in her passport clearly shows that she went directly to Kobe after landing at Tsuruga.

To confirm this, I checked the list of Jewish refugees staying in Kobe, which was prepared on August 31, 1941 by Hyogo Prefecture.

I found Rischel's name. It said that she was a German citizen arriving in Japan on March 23, 1941. Her provisional address was 5-16 Yamamoto-dori 2-chome, Kobe. She was an eighteen-year-old student.

Yamamoto-dori, Kobe ward, is now Yamamoto-dori, Chuo ward, and was known then as the temporary living quarters of Jewish refugees who came and went one after another. It seemed that Rischel was among them.

Based on the information I obtained from Rabbi Kotler, I have made a rough outline of Rischel's life, but I can't deny that there are a few things that I still wonder about. For example, one detail from Rabbi Kotler that left a strong impression on me was that Rischel had contracted tuberculosis due to her hard life in Shanghai. However, she was fortunate enough to live to be ninety-two. In 1947, she moved to Lakewood, New Jersey, and supported her husband and her father-in-law, both rabbis, in developing the town into one of the largest predominantly Jewish municipalities in the United States. When the Kotlers first moved there, its population was about 10,000, but they established a seminary that attracted students from Israel as well as the United States, thus helping to transform Lakewood into a town that now boasts a population of over 130,000.

On July 17, 2015, Rischel closed her long and eventful life. Her passing was widely lamented. At her funeral two days later, the town of Lakewood was filled with black robes as seminary students mourned her death.

"While she was alive, my mother told us children hundreds of times about the kindness of the Japanese ambassador. No matter how much she thanked him, it seemed she felt unable to thank him enough. It is true. Without that visa, this town would not exist today," Rabbi Kotler said.

Now, he wants to express his family's gratitude to the surviving relatives of Yoshitsugu Tatekawa if he can meet them.

I wanted people to know the story of the Japanese diplomat with a military background and the Jewish woman whom he saved. I posted the story on my

Rischel in her last years

Facebook page, secretly hoping that some media might pick it up. The two newspapers that covered the Nei visas, which I discovered, showed some interest, but in this case, they chose not to write about it because they thought the Tatekawa visa was different in nature from the Sugihara and Nei visas, and thus would not qualify as a "visa for life."

It's a good story, but ... Just when I was feeling disappointed, the face of a media person came to mind. I immediately sent him an email and he replied that he would be happy to help.

This was Mr. Yosuke Watanabe, the New York bureau chief of *Kyodo News*. I had met him several times before through my research activities. He had just been transferred to New York at the beginning of this year, and

Lakewood was within his beat, so to speak. In spite of the many restrictions imposed by the COVID-19 pandemic, Mr. Watanabe took a taxi to Lakewood, a one-and-a-half-hour ride, to see Rabbi Kotler. An article based on this visit was published in various newspapers in Japan shortly afterward. (The photograph is from the *Niigata Nippo* of July 20, 2020.)

Article about Yoshitsugu Tatekawa and Rabbi Kotler in *Niigata Nippo*

This media coverage had a great effect, and the ambassador of the Japanese Consulate General in New York, Mr. Kanji Yamanouchi, was invited to meet with Rabbi Kotler. This was the second visit to Lakewood for Mr. Watanabe, who accompanied the ambassador. Naturally, a second article, with a photo of Rabbi Kotler and Ambassador Yamanouchi, graced the pages of each newspaper in Japan. (Photograph courtesy of Rabbi Kotler.)

Ambassador Kanji Yamanouchi with Rabbi Kotler

Now, I must turn to the other main character of this chapter, Yoshitsugu Tatekawa.

If you are interested in history, especially military history, you may know him as a hero who, as a scout commander during the Russo-Japanese War, infiltrated deep into the enemy's camp with five men, and brought back valuable information. His exploits became widely known through the publication of *Tekichu Odan Sambyaku Ri* (Three Hundred Miles Across Enemy Territory), an account by Minetaro Yamanaka. The book became a huge bestseller in the early 1930s. It is said to have especially enchanted young boys. Tatekawa rose steadily through the ranks of the Army thanks to his service. However, after the February 26 Incident, an attempted coup by young military officers in 1936, he was placed on reserve because he was suspected for "involvement" in a series of military actions, including the Manchurian Incident.[1] In other words, he was removed from the path of an elite military officer.

Yoshitsugu Tatekwa when he was a lieutenant general of the Japanese army (left); the book, *Three Hundred Miles Across Enemy Territory,* published in 1931 (right)

---

1   The Manchurian Incident was an armed conflict between Japan and the Republic of China that began on September 18, 1931, when the Kwantung Army blew up the tracks of the South Manchurian Railway, which had been transferred to the Empire of Japan during the Russo-Japanese War, at Liujiao Lake in the suburbs of Mukden (now Shenyang), Republic of China. It led to the occupation of all of Manchuria (northeastern China) by the Kanto Army and the conclusion of the Tanggu Agreement on May 31, 1933.

However, when Yosuke Matsuoka took office as minister of foreign affairs in July 1940, he appointed Tatekawa as ambassador to the Soviet Union. At this time, Matsuoka carried out an unprecedented personnel move, ousting more than forty major diplomats and appointing members of Parliament and military officers as the new ambassadors. Tatekawa was one of them. However, was it really beneficial for him to change careers from soldier to diplomat?

In this era, the world was in a state of flux. For Japan to compete with the United States and the United Kingdom, relations with the Soviet Union had to be emphasized, and the post of ambassador to the Soviet Union was the most important one to Foreign Minister Matsuoka.

"I know I will have to make many demands on you, but it is for the sake of our country. I look forward to working with you, Mr. Tatekawa."

At a farewell party held prior to Tatekawa's departure for the Soviet Union, Matsuoka reportedly squeezed Tatekawa's hand.

Six months later, on April 13, 1941, the Soviet-Japanese Neutrality Treaty was signed in Moscow. The signatories on the Japanese side were, of course, Foreign Minister Yosuke Matsuoka and Ambassador to the Soviet Union Yoshitsugu Tatekawa. It is not difficult to imagine the strong bond that must have existed between the two at that time. (I am not a historian, so I do not know the details.)

Just a month before the signing of the Soviet-Japanese Neutrality Treaty, a young Jewish woman, Rischel, came to the Japanese Embassy in Moscow where Tatekawa was staying. He issued her a transit visa to Japan. The visa is shown in the photograph (P. 105), and if you look closely, you can see that the issue number, date, transit point, and Tatekawa's signature are handwritten, but the rest is stamped. This was also the case with the Sugihara visa.

However, there were many comments and suggestions about this visa, especially Tatekawa's signature, after an article was published concerning its appearance on several papers. Some said that it was inconceivable that the ambassador himself would respond to a young woman who came to the embassy after it was closed, that the visa was probably issued by an ordinary staff member in the normal course of issuing visas, that there was no proof that the visa was issued from a humanitarian standpoint, and that we should be suspicious that it might have been forged.

Certainly, we can presume that the one who prepared this visa was not Tatekawa himself, but a person who worked under him, because it is unrealistic that the ambassador himself would handle such clerical work.

Frankly speaking, I do not have any clear evidence to refute these criticisms. However, I don't see any exaggeration in Rabbi Kotler's claim, "My mother told us this story hundreds of times." There is no reason why he should have to make up a story.

Returning to the historical record, what measures did the Japanese government have in place to deal with Jewish refugees at that time?

Already on November 11, 1938, Hachiro Arita, then minister of foreign affairs, issued a directive to the heads of diplomatic missions abroad, stating the policy of banning Jewish refugees from entering Japan and transferring them to Shanghai.

Later, on September 13, 1940, a notification from the Director General of the Security Bureau of the Ministry of the Interior effectively placed the issuance of visas under the control of the Ministry of the Interior. The notice, "Regarding the Preliminary Investigation of Visas for European Refugees," was directed to the Director General of the US Bureau of the Ministry of Foreign Affairs.

Moreover, the restrictions on the issuance of visas were further strengthened by a directive issued by newly appointed Foreign Minister Matsuoka on October 10, 1940, entitled "On the Treatment of Visas for Foreign Displaced Persons." Its contents strongly reiterated the requirement that even transit visas must be limited to a period of ten days in Japan, and that a boarding pass to the final destination and entry procedures must be completed prior to allowing the holder's entry into the country.

Tatekawa's arrival in Moscow came at a time when the pressure on Jewish refugees was tightening. He must have been preoccupied with the Soviet-Japanese Neutrality Treaty, and he probably could not have foreseen the Jewish refugee problem that awaited him.

As the year 1941 opened, telegrams began to flow frequently between the Ministry of Foreign Affairs, Ambassador Tatekawa, and Acting Consul General Saburo Nei. The following is a chronological account of their sequence. Highlighted in bold are the telegrams the content of which will be given in full below.

- February 1: Ambassador Tatekawa to Foreign Minister Matsuoka (no. 2619)
- The same day: Ambassador Tatekawa to Foreign Minister Matsuoka (no. 2625)
- February 3: Ambassador Tatekawa to Foreign Minister Matsuoka (no. 2774)
- February 6: Ambassador Tatekawa to Foreign Minister Matsuoka (no. 3065)

- February 8: Foreign Minister Matsuoka to Ambassador Tatekawa (no. 3659)
- February 8: Deputy Consul General Nei to Foreign Minister Matsuoka (no. 3252)
- February 10: Foreign Minister Matsuoka to Deputy Consul General Nei (no. 4161)
- February 12: Ambassador Tatekawa to Foreign Minister Matsuoka (no. 3596)
- February 21: Deputy Consul General Nei to Foreign Minister Matsuoka (no. 4421)
- February 22: Ambassador Tatekawa to Foreign Minister Matsuoka (no. 4594)
- February 26: Foreign Minister Matsuoka to Deputy Consul General Nei (no. 6067)
- March 5: Ambassador Tatekawa to Foreign Minister Matsuoka (no. 5754)
- **March 7: Foreign Minister Matsuoka to Ambassador Tatekawa (no. 7281)**
- March 9: Foreign Minister Matsuoka to Ambassador Tatekawa (no. 7536)
- March 14: Ambassador Tatekawa to Provisional Foreign Minister Konoe (no. 300)
- **March 17: Provisional Foreign Minister Konoe to Ambassador Tatekawa (no. 283)**
- March 19: Provisional Foreign Minister Konoe to Ambassador Tatekawa (no. 287)
- March 21: Ambassador Tatekawa to Provisional Foreign Minister Konoe (no. 334)
- March 29: Provisional Foreign Minister Konoe to Ambassador Tatekawa (no. 318)
- March 30: Deputy Consul General Nei to Provisional Minister for Foreign Minister Konoe (no. 109)
- April 7: Provisional Foreign Minister Konoe to Deputy Consul General Nei (no. 85)
- **April 18: Provisional Foreign Minister Konoe to Ambassador Tatekawa (no. 401)**
- **April 19: Ambassador Tatekawa to Temporary Foreign Minister Konoe (no. 491)**

It is impossible to provide the contents of all these telegrams in detail due to the limited space available, but they all relate to the battle between the head office and the branch offices of the Ministry of Foreign Affairs over the tightening of restrictions on the issuance of visas. Let us touch upon some of them.

March 7: Foreign Minister Matsuoka to Ambassador Tatekawa (no. 7281)
Regarding Jews and Other Refugees
We will need the following documents as a countermeasure to deal with the refugees: (1) The number of Jews and other refugees to whom you have granted transit visas during the past year (by month if possible). (2) The number of people who are expected to apply for visas in the future. (3) Is it true that the Soviet Union has a policy of not permitting those refugees to leave the country after March 18? Please investigate these facts and let us know immediately. [Author's note: This instruction seems to have been a strong restraint on Ambassador Tatekawa.]

March 17: Provisional Foreign Minister Konoe to Ambassador Tatekawa (Foreign Minister Matsuoka was on a business trip to Europe at this time) **(no. 283)**
Instructions on Procedures for Issuing Visas for Transit through Japan to Refugees in Europe
As the number of refugees in Japan has reached 1,200 and is expected to increase further, the following procedures have been established for the time being. (1) The place for issuing visas shall be limited to your embassy. (2) The number of applicants who meet the requirements shall be reported to the ministry every six months. (3) The ministry will examine and inform you of the number of applicants who can be granted visas, and only those who meet the best conditions will be granted visas within this range. [Author's note: This seems to be a de facto instruction to prohibit the issuance of travel certificates.]

April 18: Provisional Foreign Minister Konoe to Ambassador Tatekawa (no. 401)
Instruction to Report on the Number of European Refugees Applying for Transit Visas to Japan

Referring to our previous message, no. 283, please send us a reply related to the second paragraph.

April 19: Ambassador Tatekawa to Provisional Foreign Minister Konoe (no. 491)
Report of the Ignoring of European Refugees Applying for Visas to Pass through Japan
As to your telegram no. 401, since the new decision is not in accordance with the actual situation, the embassy considers that it would be advantageous for Japan and the Soviet Union to ignore the applications if the visas issued by the destination authorities in Central and South America or in the destination authority are not valid as presented and the holders of these visas will not be allowed to pass through Japan. Therefore, we will not report the number of applicants.

(Author's note: The above telegrams are kept in the Diplomatic Archives of the Ministry of Foreign Affairs. Translation is mine.)

These four examples alone do not fully explain the whole process, but in short, we can see that the Ministry of Foreign Affairs wanted to suppress the acceptance of these people as much as possible. On the other hand, it is true that both Tatekawa and Nei desired to help Jewish refugees and followed their judgment as human beings to bypass the framework of the ministry's intentions.

There is no one who can testify now as to what happened 80 years ago on the night of March 8, 1941 at the Japanese Embassy in Moscow. There are no documents left that prove it. The only thing that tells the truth is the visa in Rischel's passport.

To conclude this chapter, I would like to share my personal thoughts on Yoshitsugu Tatekawa.

When we studied the Pacific War in junior high school history classes, we were told about the Manchurian Incident, the withdrawal from the League of Nations, and the Soviet-Japanese Neutrality Treaty. I was particularly impressed by Yosuke Matsuoka's speech about withdrawing from the League. The story of how he proudly announced his withdrawal, in English, to the representatives from various countries and left the conference hall really excited my boyish heart.

As for the Soviet-Japanese Neutrality Treaty, I remember being taught that Yosuke Matsuoka was the plenipotentiary of Japan, but, unfortunately,

I do not remember the story that Yoshitsugu Tatekawa signed the treaty as the ambassador to the Soviet Union. Rather, I think that Tatekawa's presence was hidden behind Yosuke Matsuoka, and neither the teachers nor the students knew about it. However, I do remember that we were taught that the Soviet-Japanese Neutrality Treaty brought great tragedy to Japan later.

In the process of writing this book, I came across references to Matsuoka and Tatekawa, and I was very surprised to learn that these two people had a fateful relationship during Japan's modern history.

Moreover, in those days approaching April 13, 1941, the day the Soviet-Japanese Neutrality Treaty was signed, Tokyo and Moscow were engaged in a heated exchange over the Jewish refugee issue. The two men must have been spending every day together in Moscow at that time. Did they only talk about the treaty, or did the Jewish refugee issue also come up?

A year later, in March 1942, Tatekawa was called back to Japan for a short diplomatic stint of less than a year and a half. The first post that awaited him was that of a general manager of the Taisei Yokusankai, the Imperial Rule Assistance Association, a symbol of militarism, followed by serving as head of the Dai Nippon Yokusan Sonendan, an affiliated organization. I think it was this final stage of his life that made him despondent.

According to his biography, *Wreckage: Enemy Crossing Three Hundred Miles: The Life of Chief Scout Tatekawa*, written by Kinya Nakajima, on August 9, 1945, when headlines announced that the Soviet Union had broken the Soviet-Japanese Neutrality Treaty and invaded Japan, Tatekawa put down his newspaper and meditated. As a diplomat, he had fulfilled his mission, which subsequently brought on terrible consequences for his country. It must have been a heart-wrenching experience for him. One month later, on September 9, 1945 Tatekawa passed away.

The other day (July 24, 2020), I visited Tatekawa's grave in Tama Cemetery in Tokyo. The area around the tombstone was clean and weed-free, but there were no signs that anyone had visited it for a long time.

I left the cemetery thinking that his efforts to save Jewish refugees while ambassador to the Soviet Union might have been a ray of light in the darkness of his final years.

Addendum

It is clear that the entries found in the travel certificates inserted on this page are all in the same handwriting, including Tatekawa's signature. We can presume

Yoshitsugu Tatekawa's grave in Tama Cemetery, Tokyo

that the one who wrote these entries was not Tatekawa himself, but a person who worked under him, because it is inconceivable that the ambassador himself would prepare such a clerical document. In a large embassy such as the one in Moscow, it is customary for the officer in charge to do the paperwork and for the ambassador to approve it. I am planning to do more research into the details to find out where the truth lies.

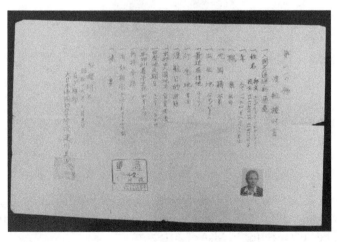

Travel certificate signed by Yoshitsugu Tatekawa. Photograph provided by the Port of Humanity Tsuruga Museum

8

Tadeusz Romer, Polish Ambassador to Japan

It would probably not be an exaggeration if I said that there are few Japanese who know about Jan Zwartendijk, the Dutch diplomat described in chapter 4.

But what about Tadeusz Romer? It would also not be an exaggeration to say that he is more unknown than Zwartendijk, except to a few researchers and others. This was the case with me until recently, because, for the past few years, my main interest has been in Zwartendijk and the Curaçao visas.

Tadeusz Romer. Photograph provided by Polish Embassy in Japan

Dr. Ewa Palasz-Rutkowska, professor of Japanese studies at the University of Warsaw, is one of Poland's leading experts on Japan. I had the opportunity to encounter her at a meeting in May of 2018.

She said, "Please read my book, *A History of Polish-Japanese Relations*, which I published in 2009. I have written about Tadeusz Romer in it."

A few days later, the Polish Embassy in Tokyo sent me a copy of a magnificent hardcover book of over 300 pages. Looking through the table of contents, I immediately turned to "Chapter 5: Cooperation in Intelligence Activities during World War II." There is a description of Chiune Sugihara as well as of Jan Zwartendijk. The detailed introduction of Tadeusz Romer's role was a true masterpiece.

"… The refugees who were able to receive visas from Sugihara arrived in Japan via Siberia. The task of receiving the refugees and arranging their accommodations was left in the hands of the then Polish ambassador to Japan, Tadeusz Romer.…"

This passage at the beginning of chapter 5 and the descriptions that followed were as moving and shocking to me as the memoir of Zwartendijk's eldest son.

I had no idea that such a fact existed! This is the most important part of the visas for life story, isn't it?

I was ashamed of my previous ignorance and wanted to include Romer in the book I was preparing, so I asked Professor Rutkowska for permission to quote from her work.

She answered, "I want to thank you for reading my book. The role of Ambassador Romer was very important. Please use my book and mention him in yours."

However, all my knowledge of Ambassador Romer is within the scope of the book, and I might have ended up quoting a lot of what is written there.

With Professor Rutkowska (in the center) on May 11, 2018

Professor Rutkowska replied that she wouldn't mind. I was grateful, but at the same time, I felt her expectations of me, which gave me strength.

Before I get to the main point, here is a brief history of Tadeusz Romer.

1894:	Born in Antonosz near Kaunas, at that time part of the Russian Empire
1913:	Began studying law and socio-political science in Lausanne, Switzerland
1919:	First secretary of the Polish Legation in Paris
1928:	First counselor of the Polish Legation in Rome
1931:	Chargé d'affaires of the Polish Embassy in Rome, after its upgrade to an embassy
1937–1941:	Temporary minister and later ambassador to the Empire of Japan
1941:	After leaving Japan, ambassador extraordinary and plenipotentiary in Shanghai for a time
1941–1943:	Ambassador to the Soviet Union
1943–1944:	Minister of foreign affairs, Polish Government in Exile (in London).
1945	After the war, moved to Canada and taught at McGill University.
1963:	Director of the Polish Academic Institute
1978:	Died in Montreal, Canada (age eighty-four)

Now let's return to the topic of how Polish diplomat Tadeusz Romer helped Jewish refugees who had escaped to Japan. Many of the refugees who landed in Tsuruga did not know where to go next and did not have enough money. So they went to Kobe to receive support from the Kobe Jewish Community (JEWCOM) and stayed there until their next move.

Actually, I'd thought that JEWCOM had taken care of the Jewish refugees during their stay there. Yet I wondered if the administrative procedures for their departure from Japan to destination countries were in order.

I can easily guess that the Jewish Community must have had a limited staff, and it would have been difficult for them to take care of everything, including accommodation arrangements.

Under such circumstances, the Polish Committee for Assistance to War Victims was established under Romer's direction. The committee started to raise funds to carry out its objectives, cooperated with Jewish organizations in Yokohama and Kobe, and set up offices in Tokyo and Kobe. Whenever a large group of refugees from Vladivostok arrived in Tsuruga, representatives of the committee went there to meet them, help them with immigration procedures, and assist them in boarding the train to Kobe.

In a letter dated February 6, 1941, Romer reported to the minister for foreign affairs of the Polish Government in Exile in London on the situation in Japan as follows:

"The influx of our refugees into Japan has presented us with a number of operational challenges. As a result of wartime financial retrenchment, the embassy, with its reduced staff, was unprepared to meet the new challenges that had fallen upon the consuls ... and on a much larger scale. ... We didn't even know in advance, in most cases, the number of displaced persons expected to arrive in Japan, and departure laws, Soviet travel regulations, foreign visa laws, and maritime navigation laws were constantly being changed. Moreover, the refugees always arrived without sufficient documentation to prove their Polish citizenship. This made it impossible for them to continue their journeys without a fundamental review and resolution of this problem. Since the refugees arrived in Japan without cash in many cases, we had to come up with a substantial amount of money to pay for their minimum living expenses, expensive telegrams, and procedures at foreign consulates."

Ambassador Romer, Mrs. Romer, and other people connected to the Polish Embassy.
Photograph provided by the Polish Embassy in Japan

Here I would like to describe in detail the Polish Committee for Assistance to War Victims mentioned above. It was set up in October 1940 at a meeting of Poles in Japan called by Ambassador Romer. The committee consisted of the following prominent members:

Chairperson: Zofia Romer, Ambassador Romer's wife
Secretary general: Mr. Klemens Zyngol (a leading business-man in Tokyo)
Treasurer: Ms. Paulina Zikmanowa (wife of the owner of the largest Polish company in Manchuria)
Director: Mr. Karol Staniszewski (secretary of the embassy)
Other members of the committee:
Mr. Alexander Piskor (head of the Polish News Agency in the Far East)
Ms. Natalia Szczesniak
Mr. Stefan Romanesco

The main activity was to raise as much money as possible, not only from Poles living in the Far East, but also from foreigners residing in Japan. They received substantial material support on several occasions from the Joint Distribution Committee in New York. In addition, when a large group of refugees from Vladivostok arrived in Tsuruga, the staff of the committee's office in Kobe met them and helped with immigration procedures. From there, they took the refugees to Kobe where the Kobe Jewish Association had specially prepared a facility to accommodate several hundred people. The small number of non-Jewish Poles coming to Tokyo was accommodated as much as possible in temporary facilities built on the embassy grounds.

However, Romer's greatest role lay elsewhere. His purpose was to have the refugees obtain permission to enter the country of their next destination. Although they had Curaçao visas, they never intended to go to Curaçao. The situation was described by Romer in a document he prepared in Tehran on October 6, 1942:

"Besides directing and supervising the entire relief effort, the Embassy of the Republic of Poland in Tokyo was directly involved in the issuance of passports to the refugees, which we took care of from beginning to end. We also acted as an intermediary between the Japanese government regarding extension of their stays, issuance of entrance and transition visas, requests of support, obtaining visas for destination countries, and so forth. Furthermore, we also were involved in the discreet registration of volunteers for the military and the sending of those volunteers to Canada and the Near East. Thanks to the efforts of the government of the Republic of Poland, a certain number of refugee visas were secured for Polish refugees in the Far East. Canada was allocated 250 visas, 80 of which were preferentially given to rabbis and seminary students in rabbinical training, 65 visas to Australia, 30 to New Zealand and 50 to Burma were also allocated. ... In addition, with the help of the embassy, we secured immigration certificates for about 400 people to Palestine. On its own, the embassy also contributed by securing visas to the United States for about 300 people and visas to Latin American countries for about 100 people."

These figures add up to 1,195 people. In short, thanks to Romer's efforts, a large number of refugees were granted permission to travel to freedom.

However, this number includes those who, despite obtaining visas, could not leave the country for some reason. One researcher found that only 827 people actually left the country.

So who was the researcher who conducted the study?

Professor Olga Barbasiewicz of Jagiellonian University in Krakow, Poland, is the person.

Professor Barbasiewicz studied Japanese history at the University of Warsaw under the aforementioned Professor Rutkowska. In the course of her research, she came across the issue of Jewish refugees fleeing Poland to Japan, which led her to the story of Chiune Sugihara's visa issuance.

Professor Barbasiewicz said, "This research is a hobby of mine, so to speak," and laughed. "I was inspired by the research of Dr. Rutkowska, whom I really admire. The number of Jewish refugees who left Japan was calculated from a list I found in the Central Archives of Modern Records in Warsaw, so it is credible."

Based on her research, Professor Barbasiewicz published a booklet last year (2019) detailing Romer's achievements. She is now the leading expert on Romer in Poland.

Professor Olga Barbasiewicz

I was, in fact, supposed to visit Poland in March this year (2020) to meet and interview Professors Rutkowska and Barbasiewicz, but the COVID-19 pandemic prevented me from doing so.

Thus, I discussed everything with Professor Barbasiewicz through Zoom before I started writing this chapter.

"By listening to your story, I have a strong feeling that Tadeusz Romer's achievements should be ranked with those of Jan Zwartendijk and Chiune Sugihara," I said. "In other words, I think that we Japanese should recognize that before the Sugihara visas, there was the cooperation of Jan Zwartendijk, who issued the Curaçao visas, and after that there were the efforts of Tadeusz Romer."

Professor Barbasiewicz agreed, saying, "You are right. I am very glad that you think so, and I am reassured. I have been writing and talking about this very same thing every chance I get. I hope that many more Japanese people will learn about this in the future."

In October 1941, when the Pacific war was just around the corner, relations between Japan and Poland were severed and the Polish Embassy was closed. As a result, the Romer family was forced to move to Shanghai. At the beginning of November, Romer arrived there as ambassador extraordinary and plenipotentiary and continued to take care of Jewish refugees there. At that time, Shanghai was under the control of the Japanese military, and the Japanese soldiers were ruthless. Their cruelty was not only directed at the Chinese but also at the people of the Allied Nations. However, the Romer family was not treated in such a way. Probably, Romer's honorable conduct as a diplomat was well known among the Japanese military.

In August 1942, with the closing of the Polish Embassy in Shanghai, Polish diplomats and consular staff from Japan, China, and Manchuria had to leave. At the last minute, fifty-four civilians of Polish nationality were allowed to leave the country, so Romer allocated forty-five seats to Jewish refugees.

He did what he had always told his family: "Jewish or not, ethnic minority or not, as long as they are Polish citizens, I have a duty to protect them."

I would like to conclude this chapter with a portion of a memoir by Oskar Schenker, a recipient of the Sugihara visa.

His deep gratitude to Ambassador Romer and the Polish Embassy strikes an emotional chord in the reader.

"I was fortunate to be among the first group to arrive in Japan via Siberia in October of 1940. I can't emphasize enough how I could not contain my excitement after a year of wandering, not knowing what tomorrow would bring, when I walked through the doors of the Polish Embassy.

"Thanks to donations from the Polish government, the Jewish-American community, the Polish Embassy staff in Tokyo, and wealthy Poles living in Japan, the refugees were guaranteed housing and living expenses.

"However, for the embassy, getting the proper destination country visas for the refugees was a major concern. It must have been a very stressful process for every member of the embassy staff. Ambassador Romer himself set the example. He was directly involved in every little thing related to the new destination and settlement of the immigrants. His daily routine consisted of constant contact with various quarters, mediation, phone calls, letters, and so forth, to the countries with which the refugees had been associated. Under his direction, all of this was done by the ambassador's secretary, Karol Staniszewski.

"Fate scattered all these people who passed through the 'gates of Tokyo' throughout the world. The last refugees who left for Shanghai are now separated by seven oceans, but united by warm memories of their time at the Polish Embassy in Tokyo and a deep appreciation for the fatherly affection with which they were surrounded. [Author's note: Oskar Schenker's name appears on Sugihara visa no. 476.]"

Ambassador Romer going to the diplomatic credential presentation ceremony in October 1937.
Photograph provided by the Polish Embassy in Japan

9

Tracking Down the 2,139 People on the Sugihara List

This chapter is an introduction to the research I conducted on a personal basis in 2018. This was not included in the original Japanese version of this book, but I decided to add it to the English version of the book on the recommendation of others.

The names of 2,139 Jews appear on the Sugihara list. However, it is said that about 6,000 Jews were saved by Sugihara visas. Where does the discrepancy between the two numbers come from?

I was asked this question by two Dutch people. One was a spokesman for the Dutch Embassy in Japan; the other was Robert Zwartendijk, the son of the Dutch consul described in chapter 4. I explained the widely accepted theory that a single visa could have included several family members. In other words, a family of three, consisting of the visa holder, his wife, and a child, is one unit, multiplied by 2,000 to get an estimate of 6,000 people.

At the time, I thought this was a reasonable interpretation, but neither of the men seemed to be convinced by it.

It is said that the theory of 6,000 people originated from *Visas for 6,000 Lives*, published in 1990 by Yukiko Sugihara, the widow of Mr. Sugihara, and that this book is the sole source of the theory. At the time of publication, research on Sugihara was still in its infancy and information was scarce, so it was unavoidable that such a situation arose.

However, as the courageous acts of Chiune Sugihara became widely admired not only in Japan but also in other countries, researchers in Japan and abroad began to pay attention to relevant details, and these two figures became the focus of their attention.

As an example, take the case of Ilya Altman, a professor at the Russian State University for the Humanities in Moscow.

Based on the records of Intourist (at that time, the state-run travel agency), which arranged the passage of Jewish refugees through the Soviet Union, he estimates that as many as 2,500 people left the Soviet Union for Japan on the Sugihara visa.

In Japan, Professor Chiharu Inaba of Meijo University wrote in his article, "Documents Related to Visas for Life and Historiography of Chiune Sugihara," that "Mrs. Sugihara estimates that the number of Jewish refugees helped by the Sugihara visa was 6,000, but this number is said to be overestimated. In fact, the number is more like 2,000 to 2,500."

I felt that I was given a homework assignment by the two Dutch men mentioned above, and I wondered what I should do. I decided on the following course of action.

Many people have expressed their opinions from various points of view, but none of them seemed to be anything more than speculation. The most reliable way, I believed, was to find out how many of the 2,139 people who received Sugihara visas came to Japan and how many family members accompanied each of them.

The first thing that came to my mind when I decided to proceed on this premise was a document in the Ministry of Foreign Affairs Diplomatic Archives that I mentioned in chapter 5. It was entitled "Regarding the Evacuation of Jews from Japan" and dated August 30, 1941. I had obtained this document in the preparatory stage of my previous book, *Visas of Life and the Epic Journey*. It was written in the name of the Governor of Hyogo Prefecture, and it contained a list of about 300 Jewish refugees who were staying in Kobe at that time. With the outbreak of war between Japan and the United States inevitable, these people, who had nowhere else to go, were forcibly sent by the Japanese government to Shanghai, which Japan occupied at that time. The list shows the nationality, date of entry, place of residence, occupation, first name, last name, and age. From the first names and ages, family relations are clearly visible. The information was handwritten and surprisingly clear, using katakana for the first and last names, and kanji for the rest of the document.

I stared at the section on family relations. *That's it!* A flash of inspiration came into my head. The main information on the original Sugihara list was nationality, first and last name, and date of visa issuance, but there were no discernible family relations because the list showed only the person who received the visa. The discovery of the Hyogo list that revealed family relationships strengthened my resolve and I set about my research. However, it was a task that required tremendous patience. I had to cross-check the names on the Hyogo Prefecture list (written in katakana, the Japanese syllabary used to phonetically transcribe non-Japanese words) with the names listed one by one in the Roman alphabet on the Sugihara list.

Hyogo list

As an example: on the first page of the Hyogo list, there are three names that appear to belong to family members.

バフラフ ヘルシ	(bafurafu herushi) 37
ハナ ヘルシ	(hana herushi) 35
ディナ ヘルシ	(dina herushi) 9

I then check the Sugihara list for similar names. Luckily, I find the following two names.

Bachrach Hersz (no. 2013)
Bachrach Hana (no. 2014)

These two names match the Hyogo list, and I am sure that they are a couple. The numbers in parentheses are the issuance numbers on the Sugihara list. Although Bachrach and Hana are a couple, they have each obtained their respective visas. The absence of the name "Dina (9)" can be interpreted as her being a child and therefore included on the visa of her father or mother.

The results of the above work were as follows:

Sugihara visa holders: 129 people
Family members of Sugihara visa holders: 61 people
Not applicable othat is, not holding Sugihara visas): 132 people

The next survey material is the "Table of Entering Jewish Refugees for the Month of October," prepared by Fukui Prefecture, dated November 27, 1940. I obtained this document after the Hyogo Prefecture list mentioned above. It is quite well preserved, and although it is entirely handwritten, it can be read very easily. The categories of the list are almost the same as those of the Hyogo list, but there is a column for the occupation of the family head, followed by the names of family members, and their relationships, such as "his wife" and "his eldest son." This extra information proves very helpful.

The procedure for the Fukui list is the same as for the Hyogo list.

On the first page, there are four names, which can be clearly identified as family members.

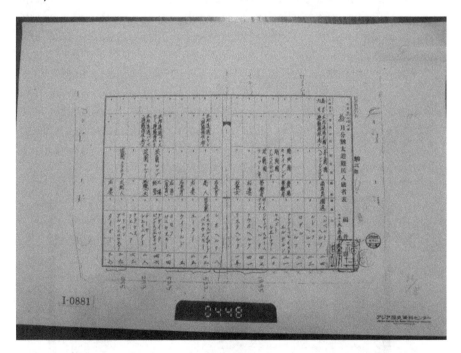

Fukui list

Laborer	ジャコブ スルリム	ヘルク	(jakobu sururimu heruku) 47
His wife	リウカ	ヘルク	(riwuka heruku) 41
His daughter	リスラ	ヘルク	(risura heruku) 15
His son	レオ	ヘルク	(reo heruku) 8

Next, I collate with the Sugihara list.

Gerc Jakob (no. 1895)

In this case, a family of four members was able to move with just one visa. The results of the Fukui Prefecture list are as follows.

Sugihara visa holders: 133 people
Family members of Sugihara visa holders: 63 people
Not applicable (other than Sugihara visas): 110 people

I was well aware that it was still impossible to see the overall trend of how many Sugihara visa holders there were from these two surveys. What was the next step? What came to mind then was the passenger lists of the ships that the Jewish refugees used to go to the United States and other third countries after they arrived in Japan.

When I inquired at the NYK Museum of History, with which I had a relationship, I was told that the museum had burned all the materials from before, during, and after the war due to its subordinate relationship with GHQ (General Headquarters of the Supreme Commander of the Allied Powers). However, it was too early to give up. I was told at the museum that the lists of passengers were available on microfilm at the National Diet Library.

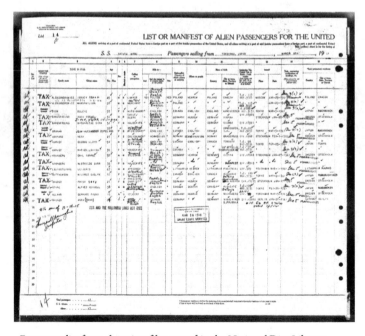

Passenger list from the microfilm stored in the National Diet Library

My visit there began the next day. As I looked at the huge amount of information on the monitor screen, it was as if I were in a small boat sailing on the Pacific Ocean. The subject of my research was the ships of the NYK Line that departed from Kobe and Yokohama between October 1940 and June of the following year. In addition, there were two Pacific routes, one to San Francisco and the other to Seattle. From the ship allocation list, which I had obtained from the NYK Museum of History in advance, I counted the number of sailings of the ships in service during this nine-month period; it totaled nearly forty for the two routes. All of them were large and excellent ships, such as *Asama Maru*, *Kamakura Maru*, *Tatsuta Maru*, *Heian Maru*, and *Hie Maru*, which were the pride of Japan at that time. The number of passengers on each trip probably easily surpassed several hundred, or even close to a thousand on each route.

Finally, the struggle with the microfilm began. More than thirty names appeared at one time on each screen. There was no point in going through them blindly. The first thing I did was to check the names on the right-hand side of the screen for "Nationality: Polish" and "Language: Hebrew." Then, I picked names I thought were likely to be there and checked them against the Sugihara list. Sometimes I was wrong, but when I was right, I clearly identified those with families. This was because the main purpose of my research was to find out how many people traveled with the visa holders. However, I couldn't concentrate for long because my eyes were getting shaky. I probably overlooked some things.

After more than a week of daily visits, the results were as follows:

Sugihara visa holders: 169 people
Family members of Sugihara visa holders: 67 people

Now, the results obtained through these three surveys are as follows.

Of the 2,139 people on the Sugihara list, 431 (129+133+169) were confirmed to have entered Japan, and these Sugihara visa holders were accompanied by 191 (61+63+67) family members. I was somewhat disappointed. The 431 people I was able to confirm represented just twenty percent of the entire Sugihara list. After so much time and hard work, only twenty percent of the list was confirmed!

However, just as I was about to become despondent, a helping hand was extended to me.

"What, you didn't know about this, Mr. Kitade? You can see the list in the archives of the AJDC, American Joint Distribution Committee, which was sent from the Kobe Jewish Association at that time."

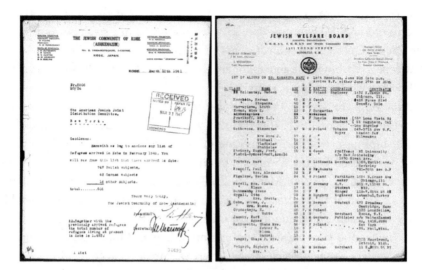

JEWCOM list

This was the news from Ms. Aya Takahashi, a resident of Vancouver, who also appeared in chapter 3. Ashamed of my ignorance, I immediately opened the AJDC website. The following two lists were treasure troves of information: "Refugees Who Arrived in Japan and Received Assistance from the AJDC" (1941) and "Jewish Refugees Who Left Japan for Safer Countries" (1941).

As can be seen from the title, the former is a list of those who landed in Tsuruga, came to Kobe and waited for assistance from the United States under the care of the JEWCOM. The latter is a list of those who were fortunate enough to leave Japan, and it is an extremely valuable document that lists each ship they were on.

With the help of these two documents, I was able to make great progress in my research, and the confirmation rate for Sugihara visa holders jumped from twenty percent to forty percent.

Furthermore, I was able to trace many additional recipients of Sugihara visas, thanks to the Embassy of the Republic of Poland in Japan. The embassy provided the Jewish refugee ledger recorded by the Polish Consulate General in Shanghai at that time.

At this stage, I felt I had reached the limit of what I could accomplish on my own. When I finally compiled the numbers, the results were as follows:

Sugihara visa holders: about 1,100 people
Accompanying family members: about 230 people

(Author's note: I use "about" because there were some uncertainties in confirming the numbers.)

A total of 1,100 out of 2,139 people on the Sugihara list equals slightly more than fifty percent, and I judged this to be substantially credible. I gave a lecture about it at the NYK museum in May of last year. There, I announced my conclusion as follows:

"Based on the above figures, and Professor Altman's comments, I believe that the number of 6,000 is still unreasonable. Instead of saying definitively that 'about 6,000' Jews were saved by the Sugihara visa, it would be better to say, 'a few thousand.' Isn't it necessary for Japan to express some kind of acknowledgement before voices of objection from outside Japan increase?"

In response, many people said they respected the effort, while others questioned why I had to go into such detail.

In a lecture he gave at the Japan Press Club in Tokyo in December of last year, Professor Altman said, "This is very different from the conventional theory of 6,000 people. But this does not mean that I deny Sugihara's great achievement."

I agree. I would like to emphasize that I have nothing against Chiune Sugihara. I very much admire him and do not have any anti-Sugihara feelings.

Aside from that, I would like to add one more major development in this chapter. As I mentioned before, when the confirmation rate reached more than fifty percent, I sent my "private Sugihara list" to some people in Japan and abroad for their reference. One of them is George Bluman, professor emeritus at the University of British Columbia, who lives in Vancouver.

"Dear Akira," he wrote, "I am very happy to receive your list. As a matter of fact, I have been conducting my own research for several years now, and a large number of your unidentified names have been identified. Please wait while I sort out and send them to you when I have time."

Professor Bluman's parents were Sugihara survivors, and his father, Nuta Bluman, was visa recipient no. 1569. I met him when I visited Vancouver in November 2012 and we have been friends ever since. I felt as if I had found a "comrade" in the pursuit of the Sugihara list.

One month later, I received the list as promised. The name of 350 people I had not yet identified had been found by Professor Bluman. Many of them were seminary students, staff, including rabbis. It is well known that several hundred yeshiva students came to the Japanese Consulate in Kaunas and that Chiune Sugihara issued a large number of visas for them. I knew about this and had been thinking of approaching Yeshiva University in New York for information.

Professor Bluman is a child of Sugihara survivors and a university professor. I take my hat off to his highly skilled research ability. When he said, "As for the information I provided, you are free to use it in your list, as long as you add the appropriate credit statement," I was profoundly moved by his generosity.

The following is a summary of the results of my research, which was further enriched by Professor Bluman's cooperation.

> Confirmed Sugihara visa holders: 1,450 people
> Accompanying family members (including brothers and sisters, nieces and nephews): 407 people (169 of whom are spouses)

If I were to draw my own conclusions from the above, they would be as follows.

(1) The confirmation rate is $1450 \div 2139 = 0.68$, which can be judged as a sufficiently credible figure.

(2) The ratio of the total of 1,857 visa holders and accompanying family members to the total of 1,450 visa holders is $1857 \div 1450 = 1.28$, which, when multiplied by the number of people on the list (2,139), equals 2,738. This represents the total number of Jews who were helped by the Sugihara visa. In reality, however, there are some Sugihara visa recipients who are not on the list, so taking these into consideration, I think that about 3,000 is the appropriate final number.

(3) In any case, the number of accompanying family members, which was the basis for the theory of 6,000, was unexpectedly small. Therefore, the argument that several family members were able to move around with one visa, which has been used in the past, should be eliminated.

Thanks to Professor Bluman's help, I now have greater results than I had expected, and I feel some achievement in my work. On the other hand, I can't deny that the words of a close friend of mine have strangely stuck in my mind: "Many people are proud of Sugihara and it doesn't make much difference whether it was 6,000 or 3,000 people. It really doesn't change the fact that Mr. Sugihara did a great job."

Indeed, the point I am making may not sit well with admirers of Chiune Sugihara. However, I think it is important to look at the facts objectively, rather than unnecessarily glorifying his actions.

To this point, I hope that my research on the Sugihara list, although not perfect, will be of some help to those involved in future research.

In conclusion, for the readers who are interested in the details of the list, I would like to invite them to visit the following webpage created by Prof. Bluman: https://personal.math.ubc.ca/~bluman/ChiuneSugiharaLists. html.

Professor George Bluman

Conclusion

As I was writing this book, I reread the "Conclusion" of my previous book, and I noticed the following two sentences:

"In the end, what happened to these seven people? The honest answer is that unfortunately, I have not been able to find out anything about them."

Needless to say, these seven people are the ones who appear in the first chapter of this book, and as detailed in chapter 3, I have found out the whereabouts of five of the seven.

It was in early 1941 that these people arrived in Tsuruga on an old Japanese ship sailing from Vladivostok. It was between 2014 and 2015 that their identities were discovered, which means that more than seventy years had passed in the interim.

I decided to trace their footsteps not because anyone asked me to do so, but because I was moved and intrigued by the photos of seven people in an old album that I happened to see.

The people around me were surprised and delighted with the outcome. Many said it is "almost a miracle."

I am happy to be able to summarize the story in this form, and it seems that I have finally reached the end of my "far" journey.

I would like to express my sincere gratitude to those who have taken an interest in my activities and encouraged me during this time.

This year, however, we were swept up in the COVID-19 pandemic. In March, I was supposed to go to Poland and the Netherlands to meet and interview the diplomats and researchers from the two countries mentioned in this book, but I was forced to cancel my trip the day before my departure. As a result, I regret that some chapters are not fully developed. I hope that someday I will be able to complete them.

Next year will be the 80th anniversary of the year when the diplomats introduced in this book made efforts in their respective capacities to rescue Jewish refugees. I hope that my modest efforts will shed some light on these people.

Akira Kitade
September 2020

List of Major References

Bandou, Hiroshi. 『日本のユダヤ人政策1931~1943』 [Nihon no yudayajin seisaku 1931–1943; Jewish policy in Japan, 1931–1943]. Tokyo: Miraisha, 2002.

Barbasiewicz, Olga. *Tadeusz Romer, Ambasador RP w Iaponii*. Vilnius: Instytut Polski w Wilnie, 2019.

『自由への逃走』 [Jiuu eno tousou; Escape to freedom]. Edited by Chuunichi-Shinbun, Tokyo: Tokyo-Shinbun, 1995.

Inaba, Chiharu. 『ヤド・ヴァシエームの丘に』 [Yad Vashemu no okani; On Yad Vashem hill]. Tokyo: Miraisha, 2020.

Kitade, Akira. *Visas of Life and the Epic Journey*. Tokyo: Chobunsha, 2014.

Nakajima, Kinya. 『残影 敵中横断三百里』 [Zanei: tekichuu oudan sanbyakuri; 150 kilometers across the enemy territory, memoirs]. Niigata City: Niigata Nippou Jigyousha, 1998.

Melamed, Leo. *Escape to the Futures*. Hoboken, NJ: Wiley, 1996.

Palasz-Rutkowska, Ewa, and Andrzej T. Romer. *Historia stosunków polsko-japonskich, 1904-1945* [A History of Polish-Japanese Relations, 1904–1945]. 2nd ext. and rev. ed. Warsaw: Biblioteka Fundacji im. Takashimy, 2009.

Paldiel, Mordecai. *Diplomat Heroes of the Holocaust*. Brooklyn, New York: KTAV, 2007.

『歴史街道』 [Rekishi kaido; Historical route] 11 (2013).

Takahashi, Aya. 『太平洋を渡った杉原ビザ』 [Taiheiyo wo watatta Sugihara viza; Across the Pacific Ocean with a Sugihara visa]. Gifu City: Gifushinbun, 2020.

Teshima, Ryuuichi. 『スギハラ・ダラー』 [Sugihara dara; Sugihara dollar]. Tokyo: Shinchosha, 2010.

Smaller, Sylvia. *Rachel and Aleks: A Historical Novel of Life, Love, and WWII*. N.p.: iUnivers, 2007.

Warhaftig, Zerach. *Refugee and Survivor: Rescue Efforts during the Holocaust*. Jerusalem: Yad Vashem, 1988.

Yamada, Jundai. 『命のビザを繋いだ男』 [Inochino bizawo tsunaida otoko; The man who issued the visa for life]. Tokyo: NHK Shuppan, 2013.

Index

Akira Kitade

Received a BA in French Literature from Keio University in 1966. Between 1966 and 2004, worked for Japan National Tourism Organization (JNTO), and was stationed in Geneva, Dallas, and Seoul. Retired from JNTO in 2004. Published several books, including *Visas of Life and the Epic Journey* (2014). Received 2017 Foreign Minister Commendation for the promotion of mutual understanding between Japan and Jewish society.

Kuniko Katz

Holds a BA in Japanese Literature from Antioch College, Ohio and an MFA in Writing from Sarah Lawrence College, New York. Writer, translator, community organizer, cross-cultural consultant, and former Japanese language teacher at Sarah Lawrence College.

Donna Ratajczak

Earned a BA in English Language and Literature from the University of Chicago and an MFA in Creative Writing from CUNY—Brooklyn College. Writer, editor, and instructional designer based in New York City.

CPSIA information can be obtained
at www.ICGtesting.com
Printed in the USA
JSHW051442100622
26950JS00003B/11